The Problem-Solver's Toolkit

A Surprisingly Simple Guide to Your Lean Six Sigma Journey

Thank you for purchasing
The Problem-Solver's Toolkit!

Please email us at contact@goleansixsigma.com with proof of purchase (a screenshot of your receipt) and we'll send you the PDF version that will allow you to access all the links!

Version 1.3

Copyright © 2018 GoLeanSixSigma.com. All rights reserved. No part of this publication may be reproduced, distributed, or transmitted in any form or by any means, including photocopying, recording, or other electronic or mechanical methods, without the express written permission of the publisher except for the use of brief quotations in a book review.

About the Authors

Elisabeth Swan and Tracy O'Rourke

Elisabeth Swan and Tracy O'Rourke are both Managing Partners at GoLeanSixSigma.com and co-hosts of the Just-In-Time Cafe Podcast — a blend of interviews, book reviews, process improvement newsmakers and helpful apps. After 20+ years of continuously improving, these two still revel in making things easier, better and more fun!

As veteran Lean Six Sigma trainers and consultants, they have worked together to make process improvement accessible to the world at large. They've collaborated to create online training, webinars, tools, templates and anything that will make life easier. They are passionate about getting stories out there to highlight the problem solvers making a difference in the world today.

Tracy and Elisabeth at a pitstop during their journey at San Diego Zoo Safari Park.

Praise for the Problem-Solver's Toolkit

Sometimes, when you're solving a problem, you just need a tool, and to know if the tool you are choosing is the right one to get the job done! Whatever continuous improvement philosophy you follow, this book will help you select the right tool, guide you on how to use it correctly, and steer you away from pitfalls and potholes along the way! And, you'll have fun following the folks at the Bahama Bistro as they use the tools to solve the problem they're having with slow lunch service! Easy to read, and easy to use, this book is another great product from my friends at GoLeanSixSigma.com!

Karyn Ross
Karyn Ross Consulting
Shingo Prize-winning Coauthor of *The Toyota Way to Service Excellence*

- - -

In **The Problem Solver's Toolkit**, Tracy and Elisabeth have put together an effective guide to help relative newcomers to Lean Six Sigma. It is a visual, easy-to-read book with a case study to demonstrate how Lean Six Sigma tools and techniques can be applied (a scenario that every reader can relate to).

Their decision to focus on the significant-few tools with the most impact benefits the reader by minimizing the risk of information overload. In addition to the visuals and case study, the book is filled with links to relevant blog posts, videos and templates. If you are in the early stages of your problem-solving adventure, pick up this fun, intuitive and easy to follow guide!

Mike Osterling
President, Osterling Consulting, Inc.
Co-Author of *The Kaizen Event Planner*, *Value Stream Mapping* and *Metrics Based Process Mapping*

- - -

Tracy O'Rourke and Elisabeth Swan have created and delivered an-easy-to-use, simple, yet thorough guide to Lean Six Sigma. Their approach to treat the journey of a Lean Six Sigma project like a travel adventure works in so many ways. They provide help via "Roadside Assistance" signs and warnings via the "Potholes and Detours" icons throughout the guide. Where readers want to dig deeper, they provide "Sightseeing and Additional References." I highly recommend this guide for anyone beginning their Lean Six Sigma adventure!

Jerry M. Wright
PE, MBA, LSSBB, LGC
CEO/President, LEANwRIGHT, Inc.
Former CEO/Chairman, Association for Manufacturing Excellence
Lean and Process Excellence Instructor, University of California,
San Diego and San Diego State University

- - -

The key word on the cover of Elisabeth Swan's and Tracy O'Rourke's new book, **The Problem-Solver's Toolkit: A Surprisingly Simple Guide to Your Lean Six Sigma Journey***, is that little adjective—"Simple"—in the subtitle. Most books written by consultants tend to be complex, full of jargon, and kind of torturous to slog through. After all, if things were simple and straightforward, why would you need consultants?*

Swan and O'Rourke have enough confidence in themselves—and respect for their readers—to lay things out in, yes, simple, straightforward, and highly accessible terms. They're with you every step of the way on your Lean Six Sigma journey offering suggestions, pointing out pitfalls, and speaking the clear, simple language of their learner/users rather than the complexification of navel-gazing consultants.

Or, to put things in more simple and straightforward terms, their book is an important contribution to the world of Lean Six Sigma and process improvement. Read it. Use it. And watch the results roll in.

John Guaspari
Author of *I Know It When I See It: A Modern Fable About Quality*; and *Otherwise Engaged: How Leaders Can Get a Firmer Grip on Employee Engagement and Other Key Intangibles*

I am excited to recommend this guide to students who are ready to begin their process improvement journey! Tracy O'Rourke and Elisabeth Swan have an incredible ability to translate intricate concepts into fun and relatable learning experiences. **The Problem-Solver's Toolkit** *allows readers to go beyond the classroom and access Lean Six Sigma concepts with engaging, smart and entertaining examples.*

Angela Miller
Program Manager, UC San Diego Extension

With **The Problem-Solver's Toolkit***, Tracy O'Rourke and Elisabeth Swan have delivered the missing link. Coming from the Innovation side of the house, I appreciate it when the process improvement side takes a more inventive approach to what is often a dry and studious topic. My clients need to innovate, but they also need to fix what's broken. This plain-spoken, good-natured, graphical journey through Lean Six Sigma is just the ticket.*

Mitch Ditkoff
CEO, Idea Champions
Author of *Storytelling at Work, and Storytelling for the Revolution*

Tracy O'Rourke and Elisabeth Swan have put together an easy to understand and engaging "travel" guide that allows any level of learner to benefit from the tools, information, and "quick tips" included. It literally walks you step by step through the choosing of a project all the way to project completion. I see using this book as a field guide to help any level of learner through process improvement. I know my copy will be (digitally) dog-eared and sticky-ridden in no time. I recommend this toolkit to anyone who is working on process improvement.

Kara Cuzzetto
Continuous Improvement Manager,
King County Financial & Business Operations Division (FBOD)

If you haven't met GoLeanSixSigma.com's problem-solving team at Bahama Bistro, you're in for a treat as the waitstaff demonstrates basic Lean Six Sigma tools while they improve their own lunch order process. This impressively accessible guide takes a user on a process improvement journey, and the Bistro team travels with you. **The Problem-Solver's Toolkit** *is a banquet of valuable tools and practical advice, all served up for users on the go!*

Dodd Starbird
Managing Partner, Implementation Partners LLC
Author of *The Joy of Lean* and *Building Engaged Team Performance*

The Problem-Solver's Toolkit *is exactly what my Green Belts need. We will always be on a process improvement journey, so how great to have a travel guide! The infographics alone are perfect teaching tools. Three cheers for Elisabeth and Tracy for providing such easy access to the building blocks of Lean Six Sigma!*

Anne Colwell
CEO, Cape Cod Child Development

Tracy and Elizabeth have hit the nail on the head with this gem. Great examples and a unique style make for a guide which is fun to read and particularly ideal as a companion for online learners. There is solid coverage of just the right tools to help you succeed with real projects rather than an overabundance of tools seldom seen or used. The writing style and subject knowledge places this guide head and shoulders above any of its competitors. Finance and operations professionals will find this a great guide for implementing Lean Six Sigma in the workplace. Share it with your co-workers! Buy a second and add it to your corporate library.

Bill Zerter
CPA, B Eng, MBA
CFO, Wolf Advanced Technology,
former CFO Wiley Publishing Global Education

The authors' approach the topic with a sense of fun and enthusiasm, providing a great high-level overview of Lean and Six Sigma tools. From how to identify opportunities for improvement all the way to putting controls in place to sustain improvements, **The Problem-Solver's Toolkit** *by Elisabeth Swan and Tracy O'Rourke is an excellent guide for anyone embarking on a process improvement journey.*

One of the most appealing aspects of the toolkit is the user-friendly layout. The clear and engaging graphics make concepts easy to understand and links to templates and additional resources allow the reader to dive deeper into specific tools. This is a great guide for anyone looking to grow their knowledgebase to become a better problem solver.

Marc Myers
Program Director, College of Extended Studies
San Diego State University

- - -

As a Lean Six Sigma practitioner I often have to check my resources to see what tool or technique might suit a particular need. For me, **The Problem-Solver's Toolkit** *acts as a personal knowledge shelf that I can reach out to when the need arises. It is well written, practical, user friendly and easily my first point of reference to check something I've forgotten since my Lean Six Sigma certification. I highly recommend it to anyone starting out on their process improvement journey and as a refresher and incredibly useful resource for those of us further along.*

Sandra Flynn
Student, Digital Education, University of Edinburgh, Scotland
Certified Green Belt, GoLeanSixSigma.com

- - -

I've been working as a specialist in the Lean Six Sigma space for the past 23 years. Through their training, consulting, blogging, podcast and now their eBook, the work of Elisabeth, Tracy and the whole GoLeanSixSigma.com Team is dramatically transforming the depth, scope and reach of Lean Six Sigma worldwide!

Bennett A. Neiman, PhD
Author of *Slay the Dragons, Free the Genie* and
The Visionary Team Planning Fieldbook

- - -

GoLeanSixSigma.com has done it again! After 5 years in quality improvement and 2 years of Lean Six Sigma training, I still have so much to learn. I have struggled with clearly documenting a PDCA. It was always a painful process. After reading this book and following their template, the PDCA documents seemed to flow much smoother. The graphics and examples explain simple concepts simply, all from the light-hearted angle of a roadtrip with friends. Reading it cover to cover can be accomplished quickly but I know I will keep coming back to reapply these tools in new ways. This book is a business staple which I use more than the stapler on my desk.

Lynne Emmons
Director of Quality Management and Compliance, Valle del Sol

- - -

GoLeanSixSigma.com has always been best-in-class with their online learning offerings. They are able to distill the topics and capabilities into an easy-to-consume and enjoyable format that makes learning both productive and fun. They have done it again by following the same recipe with this companion guide. It is easy to consume and really helps readers understand what is important to know and allows them to take this knowledge back and apply it immediately to their projects.

Kevin Hanegan
Vice President of Knowledge and Learning, Qlik

- - -

Table of Contents

About the Authors	3
Praise for the Problem-Solver's Toolkit	4
Table of Contents	10
Preface	13
Introduction	14
Steps in the Introduction Phase	15
How to Use This Book	20
Overview of Process Improvement	23
Introduction to PDCA and DMAIC	26
Lean Six Sigma Project Types	30
Introduction Phase Travel Kit — What's Inside	32
8 Wastes	33
Project Selection	37
Project Champion (aka Sponsor)	41
Improvement Team	44
Introduction Phase: Summary	45
Define Phase	47
Steps in the Define Phase	48
Define Phase Travel Kit — What's Inside	49
Project Charter	50
Voice of the Customer Translation Matrix	53
SIPOC	57
Process Walk	60
Swimlane Map	64
Value Stream Map	68
A3	71
Stakeholder Analysis	75
Involve Other People	79
Define Phase: Summary	79

Measure Phase   **82**
    Steps in the Measure Phase   83
    Measure Phase Travel Kit — What's Inside   84
       Data Collection Plan   85
       Operational Definition   89
       Takt Time   92
       Measures of Cycle Time   95
       Check Sheet   98
       Baseline Measure   102
    Measure Phase: Summary   105

Analyze Phase   **108**
    Steps in the Analyze Phase   109
    Analyze Phase Travel Kit — What's Inside   110
       Value-Added Flow Analysis   111
       Pareto Chart   116
       Histogram   119
       Run Chart   122
       Box Plot   125
       Scatter Plot   128
       Fishbone Diagram   131
       5 Whys   135
       Root Cause Hypothesis Statement   138
    Analyze Phase: Summary   141

Improve Phase   **144**
    Steps in the Improve Phase   145
    Improve Phase Travel Kit — What's Inside   146
       5S   147
       Work Cell Design   151
       Kanban   154
       Solution Selection Matrix   157
       Failure Modes & Effects Analysis (FMEA)   160
    Improve Phase: Summary   164

Control Phase **167**
   Steps in the Control Phase 168
   Control Phase Travel Kit — What's Inside 169
      Monitoring & Response Plan 170
      Executive Summary (aka Completed A3) 174
      Project Storyboard 177
      Innovation Transfer 181
      The Next Project 181
   Control Phase: Summary 182

Acknowledgments **187**

Index **189**

Preface

The idea for this book was the result of repeated requests from our learner community. They love the online training but wanted a companion guide. We started there, but then we thought, why not make it accessible for everyone? So we did!

Do we need another tool book, yes! Most reference guides are exhaustive *and* exhausting — *"Over 1000 Tools!"* There's lots of great tools out there, but a critical few essentials are often all you need. Learners in this field struggle with the sense that the subject matter has to be complicated. People think they need to study for years to get *good* at it. But that's not true! A little guidance goes a long way.

Another reason was to provide a "jargon-free" reference guide. Process improvement can get pretty technical, but it doesn't have to. The simplest explanation is the best explanation. And we don't just *tell* you how to solve problems, we *show* you with fun and inventive visuals.

What if you want to know more? We stuck to the basics, but if you're reading this you're probably the type of person who likes to explore. We appreciate lifelong learners and we've included avenues for you to go "sightseeing" when you get curious. We've got an extensive — and growing — collection of resources at your disposal.

And lastly, this book is not just a "how to," it's a "how *not* to." Things don't always go as planned, so we share the most common "potholes" and the detours around them. Yes, it's important to learn from our mistakes, but there's no reason to make *every* possible misstep. We've got work to do!

We're happy to finally deliver on this — and we hope you enjoy the "journey." Our mission is to make it easy for everyone everywhere to build their problem-solving muscles. Enjoy!

Introduction

Before we hit the road we'll need to agree on a few things. We'd like to give you tips on how best to use this book. We want to give you an idea of what's to come and introduce you to your roadside companions from the Bahama Bistro.

Once you've gotten the lay of the land you might want to clarify which problem to focus on, who might support you and who you're going to ask to jump in the car.

Let's roll!

STEPS IN THE INTRODUCTION PHASE

Prepare for the Road Trip for Problem Solvers
Get ready for both the journey and the destination.

Get the Lay of the Land
Review the road map and find out where you're headed.

Learn How to Use This Book
Plan ahead and get to know the road signs.

Get an Overview of Lean Six Sigma
Get a little background on process improvement.

Get Introduced to PDCA and DMAIC
Check out the two process improvement methods of note.

Use the Introductory Travel Kit
Make use of a few tools and concepts in preparation for the Define Phase.

Road Trip for Problem Solvers

Hello Travellers! You are about to embark on your problem-solving journey. Congratulations! Let the fun begin!

Think of this as a real road trip. A journey through the world of continuous process improvement. The trip can be fun and filled with purpose. It can be life-changing and paradigm-shifting, but it can also be painful.

You can be an active participant or a "passenger." You can make this trip alone or you can find others to travel with you. Having companions enriches your experience and you get to use the carpool lanes!

Like most road trips, there's a roadmap but that's no guarantee against travel mishaps. You might get stuck behind a Winnebago for a while, hit a pothole, get a parking ticket or have a surprise run-in with the police!

We'll provide roadside assistance and help you navigate the detours. You and your companions can sight-see if things look interesting or you might need a pit stop to refresh at the Bahama Bistro. The Bahama Bistro is a Caribbean restaurant that welcomes their patrons to enjoy a tasty slice of island life.

The Staff at the Bahama Bistro

But the Bahama Bistro is more than a source of rest and refreshment. The Bahama Bistro staff are here to contribute their own case study where they apply the tools and techniques described in these pages.

By looking at the examples from the Bistro you can translate the concepts into your own work setting. The Bistro staff — illustrated on the following page — will be with you along the way as they work to solve their own problems.

They will be your roadside companions providing you with examples, graphic explanations and of course the occasional snack.

What's in it for me? Is it about the destination or the journey?

It's up to you. You choose the journey, the experience and the destination. Some folks embark on the process improvement journey merely to arrive at "certification." This could lead to a "check-the-box" mentality. Learners might want to just get it done, check off certification, put it on their resume, update their LinkedIn status and be done with it.

Certification is great but should be seen as a milestone, not the destination. If you just go from point A to point B, with no pit stops, sightseeing or Bistro snacks, you might miss out. Be careful if getting the job done means missing the journey.

Marcel Proust wrote, "The real voyage of discovery is not in seeking new landscapes but in having new eyes." Don't miss the world that opens up to you. Don't miss the experiences with your peers. Don't miss the joy and learning of the journey. How you choose to experience the journey is significant. It could either change how you see the world or become a blur in the rearview mirror.

The skills you'll learn and develop along the journey will never become obsolete. Every organization, in every industry, in every country will always need experienced problem-solvers. Forever!

For a life-long learner it's the experiences that make the difference. Our hope is that you make good use of your new process improvement mindset. We want you to see the world with new eyes and use your new skills to react to that now-new world differently.

If you do that, you'll start to see people in poorly-designed processes as victims instead of perpetrators. This will change how you interact, lead and inspire the people who work in these broken processes.

Sound intriguing? Good! Let's get started. Start your journey with a sense of hope and excitement about what's to come!

Lay of the Land: Mapping Out the Journey

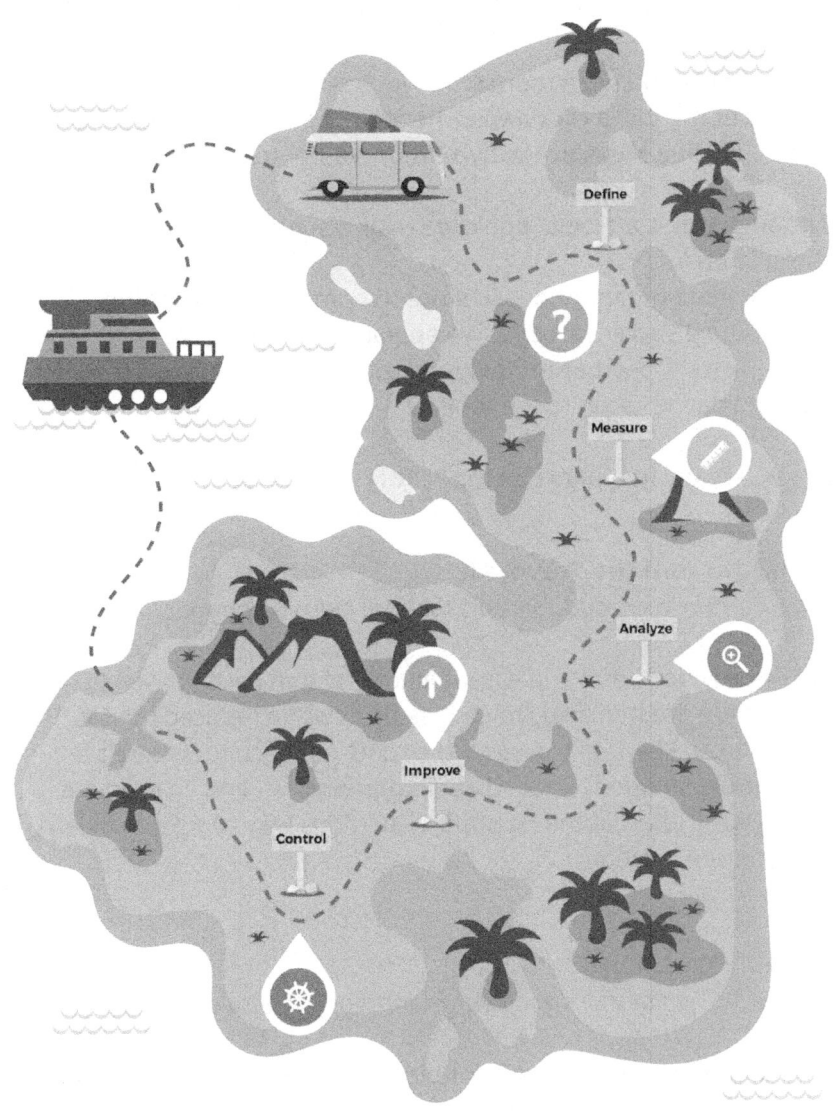

How to Use This Book

Process improvement has a seemingly bottomless toolbox. With toolboxes this full it can be daunting to find what you need. To make things easy we've created a travel kit of essentials for you to take on the road. Everything required to solve problems is right here!

If you realize you need more stuff we're ready for you. Extra resources are just a click away. The steps and tools are organized by DMAIC (Define-Measure-Analyze-Improve-Control) Phase.

Although this is a "Tools" book, we realize success isn't *just* about tools. There's leadership support, change management, strategic planning and organizational culture to name just a few of the contributing success factors. We applaud your efforts to learn more about those topics but for this road trip, we're providing you some basic guidance — on to the tools!

Are you ready for your road trip? Let's review!

From the Travel Kit
The tools and concepts that will help you on your journey.

We've provided basic and essential tools within each Phase of DMAIC. Since there are hundreds to choose from we've reduced the list. That way you can keep your eyes on the road. For each tool there's a graphic explanation — called an "infographic" — and an example from your friends at the Bahama Bistro. This way you get the idea and you see it action.

Questions
The questions each particular tool will answer.

One of the best ways to understand *why* you would use any given tool is to look at the questions it's going to answer for you. Even with the reduced toolkit you're not going to need everything here, so this list will help you determine whether to use a particular tool or not.

Roadside Assistance
The "how to" instructions for each tool.

For the tools you decide to use, we've provided some basic instructions. Some of these require templates or related webinars and for those there are links. For any tool you'd like to know *more* about, we've got the "Sightseeing" section referenced below.

Potholes and Detours
The pitfalls of using each tool along with the workarounds.

With any tool or concept, there are ways things can go wrong. We've listed the most common user issues along with ways to correct yourself and your team if you run into trouble. It's a good idea to read these *before* putting the tools into practice.

Sightseeing and Additional References
Additional references available to explore more about the tools.

Sometimes you want to know more. You might want to get out of the car, stretch your legs and investigate. We've provided a trunk full of links to templates, blogs, webinars, videos and single modules. These resources will deepen your understanding and make you smarter. Guaranteed!

Taking the Show on the Road

Before embarking on the Define Phase there are a few pre-journey stops to make.
- You'll need a brief overview of Process Improvement and the methods available.
- You're going to want to get a sense of which issues need attention and the 8 Wastes will help with that.
- You'll need to narrow down which problem to address and then you'll need someone in a leadership position to support you.
- And since it's always good to bring some friends along — you should think about building a team.
- Start your engines, please!

Overview of Process Improvement

We've all been victims of painful processes — waiting for service at a bank, getting the wrong order at a restaurant or wishing a real person would pick up the phone.

Everything organizations do for customers is the result of a process — from baking a cake, to passing a law. So why not ensure these processes run well and give customers what they want?

Process improvement means working *on* the process rather than *in* it. People get hired because they have the right skill sets. A person hired to receive and pay invoices is probably good at both those things. But process improvement requires them to step out of the process they work in and use a different skill set.

Generally speaking, when people step out of a process they're not exactly sure how to start working *on* the process. Their existing skill sets don't necessarily help them analyze and improve a process. Building new problem-solving skills is critical.

There are lots of names for process improvement:
- Lean Six Sigma
- Operational Excellence
- Process Re-Engineering
- Continuous Improvement

The list goes on. The labels are not as important as what's behind them. What matters is streamlining and simplifying processes to ensure they deliver the best products and provide the finest experiences for customers.

Pick a process with a problem and follow the roadmap to improve it. It can be difficult, but don't jump to solutions. Instead, study the process, find the root causes and implement countermeasures that address the root causes. You can do it!

Lean Six Sigma

Lean and Six Sigma are both well-known process improvement methods. Although the term "Lean" was coined in the 1990s, the thought process is traceable to the Toyota Production System (TPS) in the 1940s. Six Sigma emerged from Motorola in the eighties. Both Lean and Six Sigma are robust approaches and toolkits for improving processes.

Both methods are based on the Scientific Method as a way to analyze processes and discover root causes of process issues. Lean uses **Plan-Do-Check-Adjust (PDCA)**. Six Sigma uses **Define-Measure-Analyze-Improve-Control (DMAIC)**.

Check out the full infographic here.

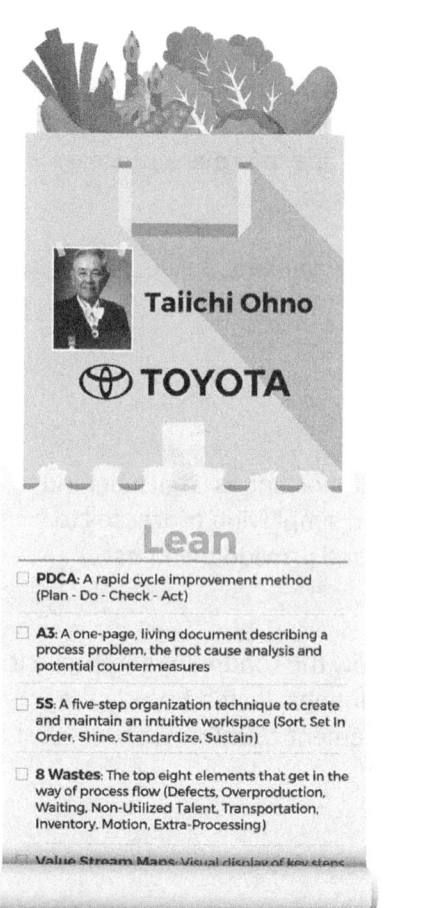

Introduction to PDCA and DMAIC

Both PDCA and DMAIC are established methods for problem-solving and root cause analysis.

PDCA

PDCA uses a four-step method and focuses on understanding the situation, analyzing root cause, implementing and testing countermeasures, making adjustments and repeating the cycle until the process improvement has been optimized.

PDCA has a long history but most people attribute Walter Shewhart as the creator. Dr. Shewhart was Dr. W. Edwards Deming's mentor and with Deming, PDCA evolved into PDSA: Plan-Do-Study-Act.

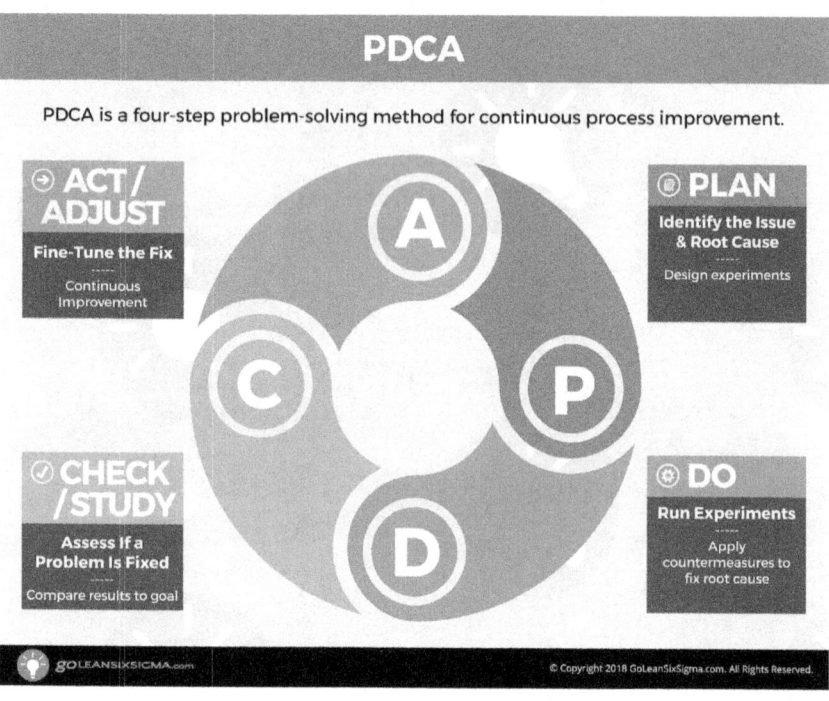

Brief History of PDCA

The detail involved with following PDCA has evolved over time. There are many schools of thought and resulting variation, but the principles and goals remain steady.

Deming's PDSA Cycle has a fascinating history. It starts hundreds of years ago with Galileo, evolves with the Shewhart Cycle and keeps refining right into the 1990s. If you are interested in learning more, there is an excellent white paper by Ronald Moen titled "Foundation and History of the PDSA Cycle."

Sub-Steps Within PDCA

The detail varies but the objective is always to build good problem-solving habits. The Toyota Production system outlines 8 sub-steps within PDCA that help you apply problem-solving skills and thinking. PDCA is front-loaded with 60%-75% of the work happening in the "Plan" step.

Plan	1. Clarify the problem
Plan	2. Break down the problem
Plan	3. Set a target we will achieve
Plan	4. Analyze the root cause
Plan	5. Develop countermeasures
Do	6. Implement countermeasures
Check	7. Evaluate process and results
Act	8. Standardize success, learn from failures, set another target

Next up, a slightly different (but similar) method to problem solving, DMAIC.

DMAIC

DMAIC is a five-step process improvement method. Like PDCA, it's an iterative improvement model. DMAIC focuses on defining the problem, quantifying the current performance, analyzing root cause, implementing improvements and sustaining the improvements with monitoring and adjustment.

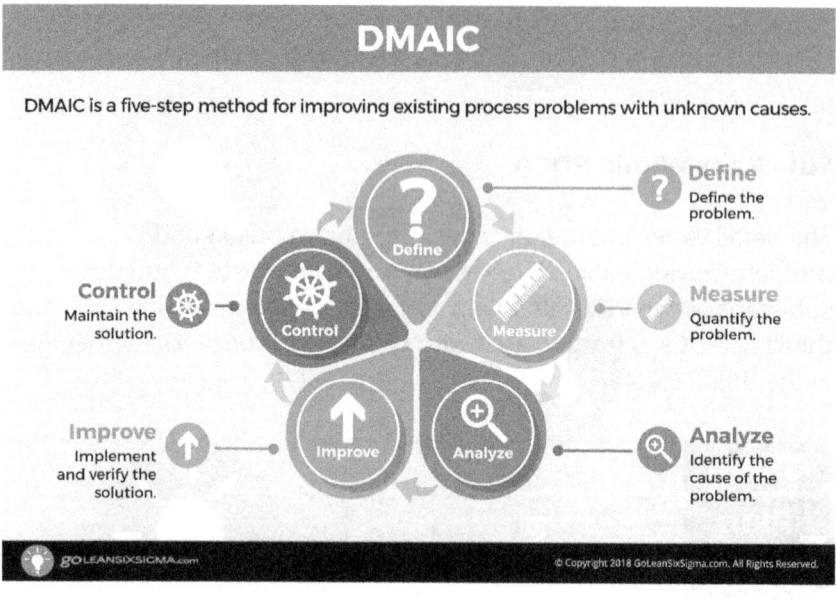

Brief History of DMAIC

DMAIC is the acronym used to define the model used in the Six Sigma method of continuous improvement. Six Sigma was founded at Motorola in the mid-80's by quality engineer Bill Smith. Working alongside Dr. Mikel J. Harry, they refined the approach to transform Motorola's culture and the quality of their products.

Steps Within DMAIC

Like PDCA, the DMAIC approach is front-loaded with methods to understand and build profound knowledge about the current state of a process within the Define and Measure phases. It covers all the bases in 5 Steps.

PDCA and DMAIC Together

Since both are based on the Scientific Method, these models are in alignment:

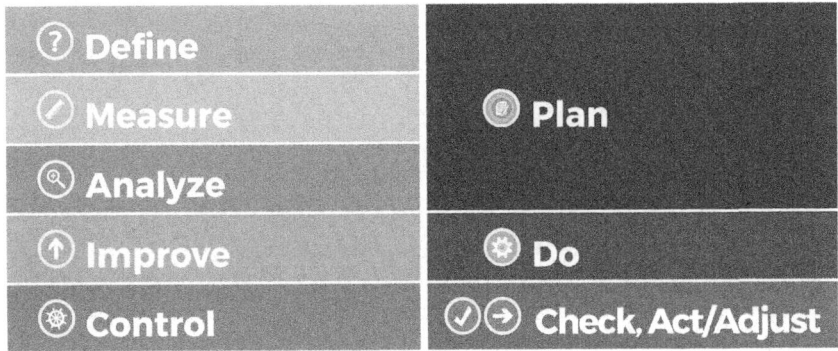

You may run into process improvement enthusiasts who prefer one camp over another...the Lean camp versus the Six Sigma camp and vice versa.

We find that viewing these as similar (but different models) is helpful. Ultimately, either of these methods will generate good results. What's key is having a framework to follow. There are many different ways to solve problems. This guide provides structure and "structure sets you free." With guidance, you are free to follow the best path for you within the basic structure.

On a deeper level, both methods — PDCA and DMAIC — require organizations to build cultures that support process change, tolerate risk and enable problem solvers to thrive. For this journey we are following the DMAIC Phases.

Lean Six Sigma Project Types

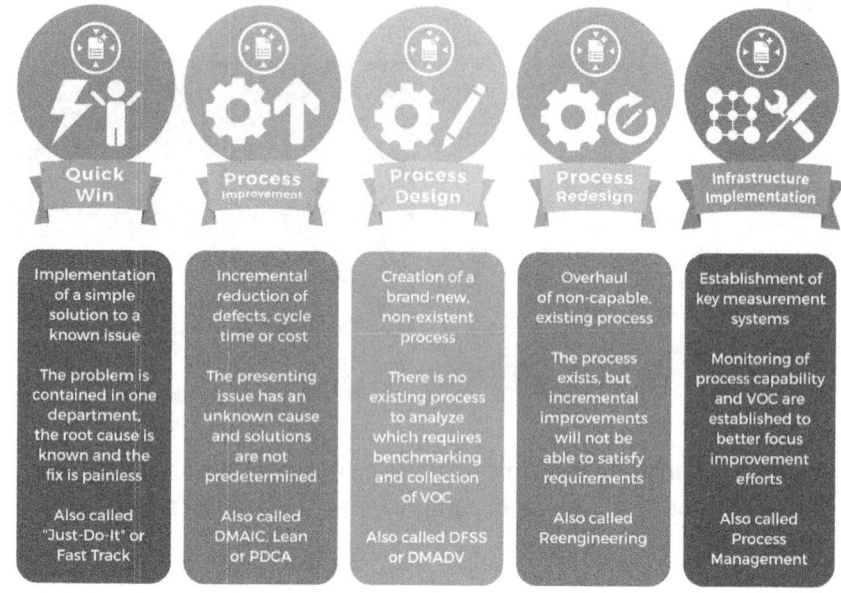

Organizations and individuals run into all kinds of problems! But not every problem is related to a process, and not every problem requires root cause analysis. This book is a guide for addressing process improvement opportunities — listed in pink above.

If you have an obvious problem and you know what to do —fix it! If you have a problem that's unrelated to a process, then you won't need this guide. This is a toolkit for *process* improvement so it begins with a process. Below are some examples of the different types of projects to help you tell the difference.

Sample projects for each approach:
- Quick Win: Stop accepting incomplete applications
- Process Improvement: *Reduce the rework when issuing licenses*
- Process Design: Invent a way to sell products
- Process Redesign: Completely overhaul the application process

- **Infrastructure Implementation:** Install an error tracking system

If there is an existing process with a problem and the root cause is unknown — then this is the guide for you! You'll need guidance to bridge the gap between the current process performance and the desired process performance. That's where this book comes in!

INTRODUCTION PHASE
TRAVEL KIT — WHAT'S INSIDE:

The 8 Wastes
The 8 Wastes are eight types of process obstacles that get in the way of providing value to the customer.

Project Selection
Project Selection is choosing a process improvement opportunity with the greatest impact and the least effort while still aligning with organizational strategy.

Project Sponsor/Champion
A Champion (Sponsor) is someone in leadership who supports the improvement team and the process being addressed.

Improvement Team
A Process Improvement Team consists of other process participants with the interest and ability to work together on a process improvement opportunity.

FROM THE TRAVEL KIT:
8 Wastes

The 8 Wastes are eight types of process obstacles that get in the way of providing value to the customer.

Defects — Efforts caused by rework, scrap, and incorrect information.

Overproduction — Production that is more than needed or before it is needed.

Waiting — Wasted time waiting for the next step in a process.

Non-Utilized Talent — Underutilizing people's talents, skills, & knowledge.

Transportation — Unnecessary movements of products & materials.

Inventory — Excess products and materials not being processed.

Motion — Unnecessary movements by people (e.g., walking).

Extra-Processing — More work or higher quality than is required by the customer.

© Copyright 2017 GoLeanSixSigma.com. All Rights Reserved.

What are the 8 Wastes?

Why cover the 8 Wastes first? Because one of the first things process improvement enthusiasts must learn to do is "see with process improvement eyes." You must learn to see waste, in order to see opportunities to improve. Most of us are so accustomed to waste that we stop seeing it. Time to change all that!

A huge focus of process improvement is to identify and remove all forms of waste from a process in order to increase efficiency, reduce cost and provide customer value. The 8 Wastes refer to a list of obstacles that get in the way of process flow and cause stagnation, the antithesis of your process improvement objectives. The list consists of Defects, Overproduction, Waiting, Non-Utilized Talent, Transportation, Inventory, Motion and Extra-Processing.

What Questions Will the 8 Wastes Answer?

- What are the non-value adding activities in the process?
- What is getting in the way of process flow?
- What is a good process area to focus on given the type of waste in the system?
- What is preventing us from delivering value to the customer?
- Which of these issues might become a good process improvement opportunity?

Example of Removing Waste

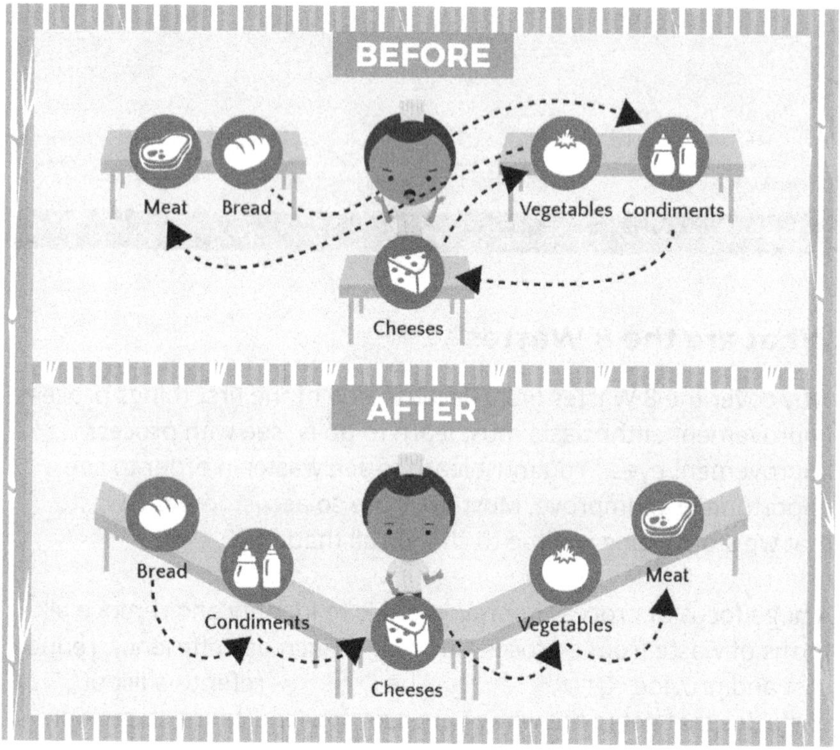

BEFORE

Meat · Bread · Vegetables · Condiments · Cheeses

AFTER

Bread · Condiments · Cheeses · Vegetables · Meat

The Bahama Bistro identified a few wastes in the sandwich preparation area. There was the waste of Transportation when staff transported the sandwich to different tables, the waste of Motion when they had to walk and reach for supplies and since this took a while, the customers experienced the waste of Waiting! Reorganizing the supplies and the layout immediately improved the flow.

Roadside Assistance
How to Use the 8 Wastes

1. Download the 8 Wastes Check Sheet template.
2. Choose a process to assess.
3. Review the examples of each type of waste.
4. Rate each waste as existing in "High," "Medium," or "Low" amounts.
5. For medium and high levels, describe that waste in the selected process.
6. Determine where to focus on reducing waste that is interfering with process flow.
7. Consider one of these issues as a potential process improvement project.

Potholes and Detours Around Them

Potholes	Detours
Assuming the 8 Wastes apply exclusively to manufacturing processes with tangible products	The 8 Wastes are universal. Assess emails, orders, applications and other units that are flowing through the process.
Not realizing that batching can lead to the waste of waiting	Be sure to assess processes that run in batches to see if you can reduce the batch size.
Assuming that overproduction only applies to tangible products	Consider things like "reply-all" on emails as a form of overproduction.

Not identifying where talent goes unutilized	Remember that requiring manager approvals is a form of non-utilized talent when others could decide.
Obsessing over the wrong wastes	Focus on the wastes that cause the most disruption to process flow.

 Sightseeing and Additional References

Template:
- 8 Wastes Check Sheet

Blog:
- Grand Daddy of Quality: Taiichi Ohno

Webinar:
- Introduction to Lean

Single Module:
- 8 Wastes Training

FROM THE TRAVEL KIT:
Project Selection

Project Selection

Project Selection is choosing a process improvement opportunity with the greatest impact and the least effort while still aligning with organizational strategy.

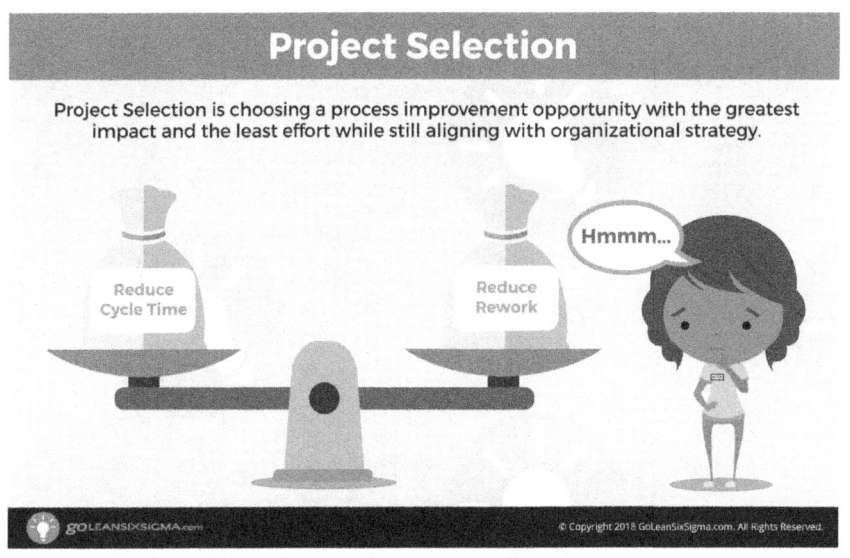

What is Project Selection?

Project Selection involves determining which process issue would make a good Lean Six Sigma project. Selection is based on the impact it could have on customer satisfaction, potential time savings, potential cost savings and how manageable the effort would be while still aligning with organizational strategy.

What Questions Will Project Selection Answer?

- What existing process is not performing as well as it should?
- What's the measurable problem?
- How long has the problem been happening?
- What's the measurable target that if reached, would indicate the project is successful?
- What's a problem that will require the least amount of effort to fix and provide the most positive impact?

Example of Project Selection

"Did you know that for the past 6 months our lunch orders are averaging 27 minutes to deliver? We're losing customers!"

"This will be an excellent project. We need to get that down to 20 minutes by the start of the summer."

Impact Effort Matrix of Potential Projects

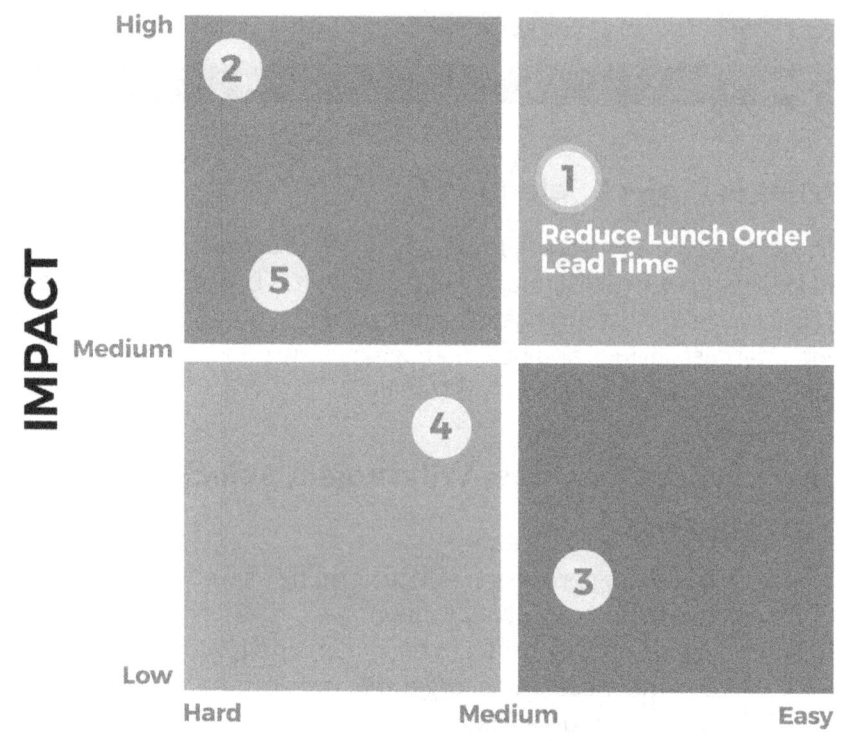

IMPACT (High / Medium / Low) vs **EFFORT** (Hard / Medium / Easy)

- ② High impact, Hard effort
- ⑤ Medium-High impact, Medium effort
- ① **Reduce Lunch Order Lead Time** — High-Medium impact, Easy effort
- ④ Low-Medium impact, Medium effort
- ③ Low impact, Easy effort

The Bahama Bistro decided to focus on the issue of late lunch orders. This is a key process since it involves almost everyone at the Bistro and it has an immediate impact on customers. Some customers have to get back to the office as soon as their food arrives. This process has universal support and it looks very doable, so it's time to fix this problem!

Roadside Assistance
How to Select a Project

1. Download the Project Screener.
2. Watch the "Getting Started with Your Green Belt Training and Certification" Webinar.
3. Fill in the Project Screener and share with your Sponsor.
4. In addition to the Project Screener, you can also use the Impact Effort Matrix to plot the relative impact vs effort involved with each project idea.

Potholes and Detours Around Them

Potholes	Detours
Choosing a process that does not currently exist and needs to be created	Make sure the focus is on an existing, repeatable process.
Assuming there is "no process"	Just because a process is not functioning well doesn't mean there's "no process."
Not having any way to measure the process performance	Make sure there is one main way to measure the performance such as cycle time, % of defects, etc..
Not providing a measurable goal	Make sure the Goal Statement includes a target level for the measurable problem such as a lower cycle time or % of defects.

Stating the goal as the solution	Make sure the goal statement is focused on the measurable target and not how you expect to reach it.
Picking a process issue with a known root cause and obvious solution	This is what's called a "Quick Win" and does not require DMAIC. It's known as a 'Just Do It' so go ahead and do it, but you won't need DMAIC when you do."
Choosing a complex process issue that involves multiple departments	Choose something meaningful and manageable so you have a good chance of success

Sightseeing and Additional References

Templates:
- Project Screener
- Project Selection Guide
- Impact Effort Matrix

Blog:
- The 3 Stages of Project Selection Maturity and How they Help You Achieve Project Success

Webinar:
- Getting Started With Your Green Belt Training and Certification

HELP WITH THE TRAVEL KIT:
Project Champion (aka Sponsor)

What is a Project Champion (Sponsor)?

A Project Champion or Sponsor is someone in a leadership position who helps a Green Belt, Black Belt or Team Lead secure resources and overcome departmental barriers in pursuit of project goals. This person has "skin in the game" meaning they care about the process being improved and regularly meet with and support team leads.

What Questions Will Selecting a Project Champion (Sponsor) Answer?

- How will the team find the resources they need to improve the process?
- Who will represent the team in leadership?
- Who will help the team overcome barriers to progress?
- Who will help the team find necessary data?
- Who cares about ensuring this particular process is improved?

Example of a Project Champion (Sponsor)

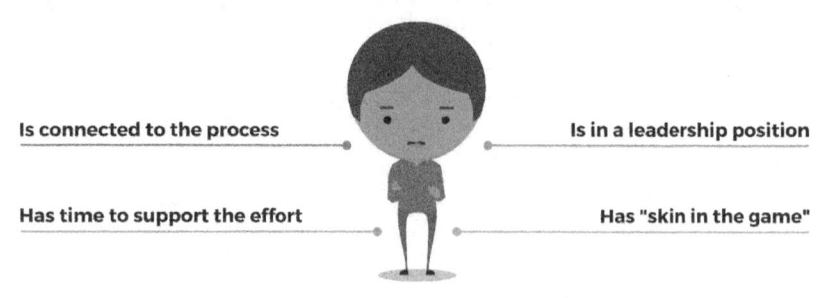

- Is connected to the process
- Has time to support the effort
- Is in a leadership position
- Has "skin in the game"

Once they selected the project, they realized it might involve changes in the entire restaurant. The leadership person with the most "skin in the game" is the Bistro Owner. The good news is that he's game to be the Project Champion (Sponsor).

Roadside Assistance
How to Select a Champion (Sponsor)

1. Assess all the people in leadership positions associated with the processes in which you participate.
2. Determine which of them has the most interest in process improvement.
3. Determine which of them has time to meet with you and play the role of Champion (Sponsor).
4. Meet with the best candidates.
5. Ask them whether or not they are interested in supporting your process improvement efforts.
6. Go with the "best fit" given your work processes, their availability and interest.

Potholes and Detours Around Them

Potholes	Detours
Champion (Sponsor) is lacking the authority to potentially remove project barriers	Make sure the person has enough positional authority to assist the team when they need it.
Champion (Sponsor) is lacking the time to support the team	Let them know the time commitment for a Champion (Sponsor). An example would be, "I expect to meet or have a call with you for ½ to 1 hour per week."
Champion (Sponsor) is lacking familiarity with the process	The Champion (Sponsor) must have a good understanding of the process being improved.

Sightseeing and Additional References

Webinar:
- How Leaders Successfully Support Lean Six Sigma Projects

HELP WITH THE TRAVEL KIT:
Improvement Team

Elisabeth	Tracy	Sean	Scott	Julian
Shift Manager	Server	Busboy	Chef	Champion
Team Lead	Team Member	Team Member	Team Member	Bistro Owner

Processes tend to cross functional boundaries and involve different groups of people. Great discoveries happen during this kind of work when connecting with other people. Your work brings you in contact with colleagues you may not regularly interact with and by engaging them you come to understand the process better.

When you ask others to join you, they'll be on the journey too. You can review what you know with them or give them a link to some free training so they can get up to speed, so to speak.

The great thing about engaging with others is that it reduces the odds that you'll have to work alone. Assemble a team and invite them to join the DMAIC road trip. You and your team can enjoy pit stops at the Bahama Bistro for more fun and better results!

Introduction Phase: Summary

Are you ready for the Define Phase? Choose your process challenge, find a Champion and start making friends. The best way to learn is by doing, so pack everybody in the car and let's go!

Introduction Phase Challenges

- Finding good improvement opportunities
- Screening out low potential project ideas
- Making sure there is leadership support
- Enlisting a sponsor for the potential project
- Finding potential team members
- Increasing organizational awareness of process improvement

Introduction Phase Best Practices

- Use the 8 Wastes Check Sheet to uncover improvement opportunities.
- Choose a project that is focused on your day-to-day activities.
- Don't proceed with a project until you have a Project Champion/Sponsor.
- Enlist team members familiar with the process.

Journey Journaling

How are you doing? Did you pack enough clothes? One thing that helps as you use this guide is to ask yourself a few questions at the end of each phase:

- Did the 8 Wastes help you see some opportunities?
- Do you feel like you have a good process problem to work on?
- Are there people to support you and work with you?
- What are some lessons learned?
- What would you do differently next time?

Introduction Journey

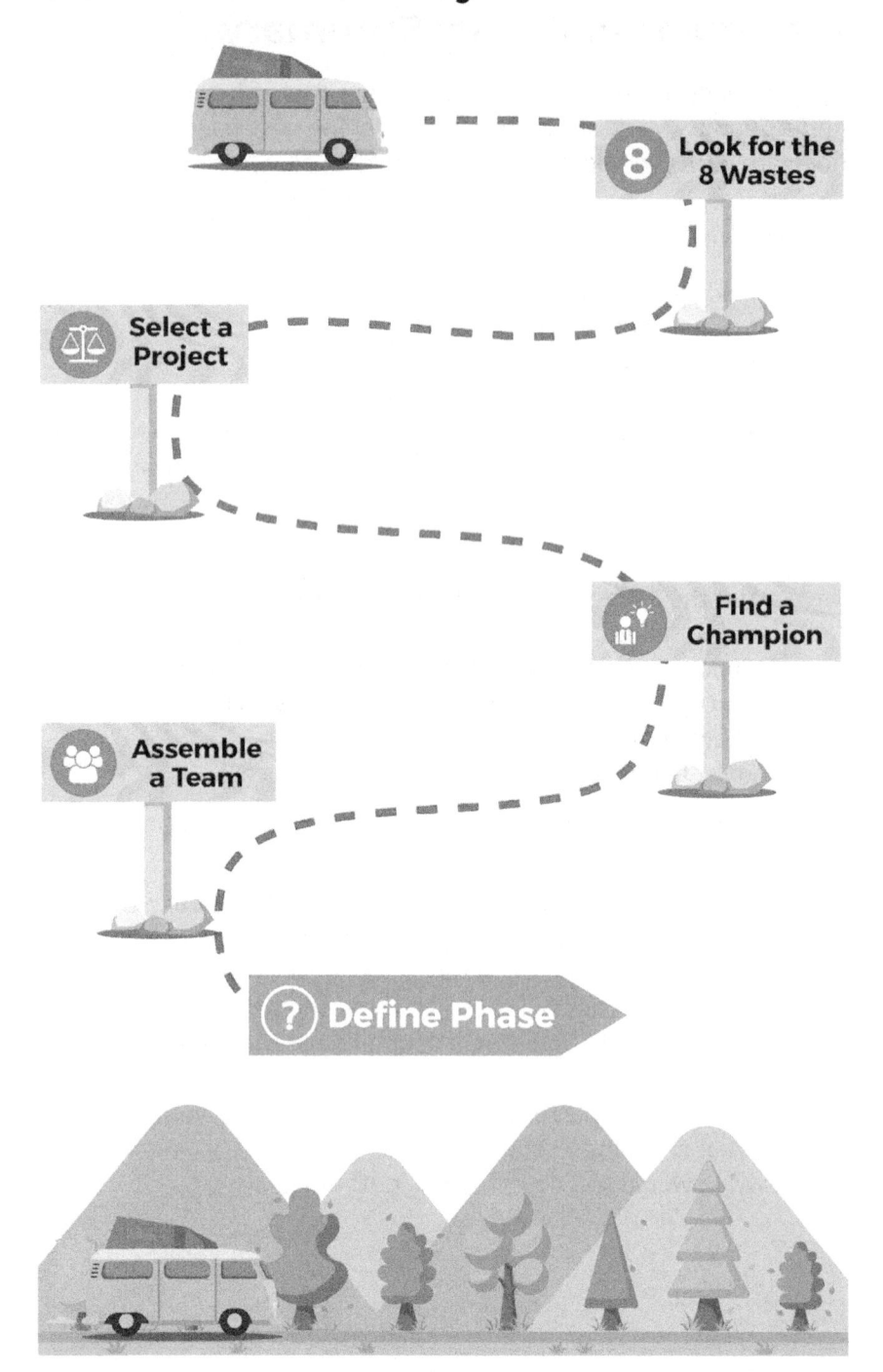

8. Look for the 8 Wastes

Select a Project

Find a Champion

Assemble a Team

? Define Phase

Define Phase

The first stop on your roadtrip is the Define Phase. Starting a journey is typically full of excitement and a little bit of anxiety about where you're headed. Having a plan helps!

As with any trip, setting the course is important. You will discover back roads and undoubtedly change your route, but you need to establish a destination. As the old saying goes, "if you don't know where you're going, any road will get you there." That's why you'll be selecting a process, a problem and a goal before heading out.

Good luck!

STEPS IN THE DEFINE PHASE

Create the Project Charter

Determine which problem is being addressed, what process is involved, who will be working on the project, what the team goal is and the eventual impact of success.

Interpret the Voice of the Customer

Determine the different customers of the process, what they have to say about the process and what that means in terms of process requirements.

Understand the Current State

Become a student of the process and work to build profound knowledge of the existing process.

Develop Project Communication

Consider all the people and groups who could be impacted by or have an impact on the success of the project and figure out how you plan to keep them in the loop.

DEFINE PHASE TRAVEL KIT — WHAT'S INSIDE:

Project Charter
A Project Charter is a living document outlining the issues, targets and framework of a process improvement effort.

Voice of the Customer Translation Matrix
The Voice of the Customer Translation Matrix turns vague comments into measurable customer requirements.

SIPOC
A SIPOC is a high level view of a process.

Process (Gemba) Walk
A Process (Gemba) Walk is an informational visit to a workplace that follows the "thing" or unit going through the process.

Swimlane Map
The Swimlane Map displays the process flow in separate lanes based on the group performing the step.

Value Stream Map
A Value Stream Map displays the high level process steps along with key process data.

A3
An A3 is a one-page report on the background and current state of a project.

Stakeholder Analysis
Stakeholder Analysis is the process of understanding who has a vested interest in a change effort and working with them to ensure success.

FROM THE TRAVEL KIT:
Project Charter

Project Charter

A Project Charter is a living document outlining the issues, targets and framework of a process improvement effort.

Problem Statement	Business Case	Goal Statement	Timeline	Scope	Team Members
The problem captured in the form of a measurement.	The business reasons for doing the project.	The target of the process measurement.	When each project phase will be completed.	What's in and what's out of the project.	The people who will participate in the project.

© Copyright 2017 GoLeanSixSigma.com. All Rights Reserved.

What is a Project Charter?

The Project Charter is a living document that outlines a process improvement project for both the team and leadership. Teams use the charter to clarify the process issue being addressed, the reason for addressing it and what "success" looks like for those working on it. It's also used to clarify what's not being addressed. It is the first step in a Lean Six Sigma project and is periodically reviewed and refined throughout the project.

What Questions Will a Project Charter Answer?

- What problem are we trying to solve?
- Why is it important?
- What's the goal?
- How much of this process are we going to tackle?
- What are the first and last steps in the process?
- What's the high-level timeline for completing this project?
- Who's on the team?

Example of a Project Charter

Lunch Order Cycle Time

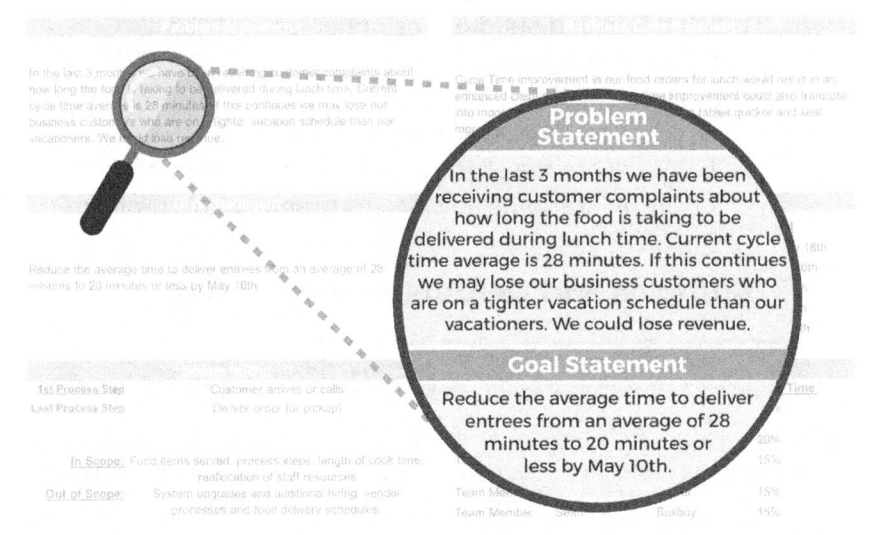

Problem Statement
In the last 3 months we have been receiving customer complaints about how long the food is taking to be delivered during lunch time. Current cycle time average is 28 minutes. If this continues we may lose our business customers who are on a tighter vacation schedule than our vacationers. We could lose revenue.

Goal Statement
Reduce the average time to deliver entrees from an average of 28 minutes to 20 minutes or less by May 10th.

[Download Example] Since the Bahama Bistro exists to provide customers with a wonderful experience, improving the lunch service is in total alignment. The team worked hard to outline exactly what the project was about and who was on the team. Everyone on the team, including the Champion, has a copy!

Roadside Assistance
How to Create a Project Charter

1. Download the Project Charter template.
2. Enter the problem statement.
   a. Name the process being addressed (Application Processing, Product Delivery, etc.).
   b. State the current severity of the problem (# defects, minutes to process, etc.).
   c. Indicate the impact on the organization (loss of customers, increased costs, etc.).
3. Enter the Goal Statement.

      a. Use the same unit and measure as the Problem Statement (# defects, minutes to process, etc.).
      b. State the baseline, state the target and when you expect to reach the target.
   4. Enter the first and last step in the process under "Scope."
   5. List what is in and out of Scope under "Scope" (job descriptions, software, etc.).
   6. Describe the Business Case.
      a. How long has this been an issue?
      b. What are the all the impacts to the business?
      c. What are some advantages to solving this problem?

Potholes and Detours Around Them

Potholes	Detours
Including a root cause or a solution in the problem statement	If the root cause and solution are clear, this is probably a Quick Win — select a new project.
Blaming a person or department in the problem statement	Even if it's true this is process improvement, not people improvement. Focus on the process.
Referencing something without a measure such as "Efficiency, Streamlining or Timeliness" in the Problem and Goal Statement	Determine the specific units and metric that are best suited to measuring the process.
Lacking a project Sponsor or Champion in the Team Members section	Find someone in leadership to support the project or find a different project.
Having multiple objectives	Don't try to improve cycle time *and* reduce defects — pick one.
Targeting perfection	Make the goals realistic. Don't let perfection be the enemy of "better."

| Working toward weak goals | Make the improvement target meaningful. Otherwise, the effort won't be worth the time. |

Sightseeing and Additional References

Templates:
- Project Charter
- Goal Statement Builder

Blog:
- 3 Important Factors to Consider to Launch a Successful Lean Six Sigma Project

Single Module:
- Project Charter Training

FROM THE TRAVEL KIT:
Voice of the Customer Translation Matrix

Voice of the Customer Translation Matrix

The Voice of the Customer Translation matrix turns vague comments into measurable customer requirements.

Customer Comment	Identifying the Issue	Customer Requirement
What are they saying?	What's the priority?	What's the measurable target?

goleansixsigma.com © Copyright 2017 GoLeanSixSigma.com. All Rights Reserved.

What is a Voice of the Customer Translation Matrix?

The Voice of the Customer (VOC) Translation Matrix helps teams take customer comments, determine the underlying issues represented by those comments and use the information to develop measurable customer requirements. The goal of this tool is to translate often vague comments into something concrete so the team can focus their efforts to meet these customer requirements.

What Questions Will the Voice of the Customer Translation Matrix Answer?

- What do the customers of the process care about?
- What do the people and groups who receive the goods and services of the process say about their experience?
- What are the underlying issues based on their comments?
- Based on those issues, what are the measurable requirements?
- How would we measure whether or not we were meeting customer requirements?

Example of a Voice of the Customer Translation Matrix

Customer Comment (What Are They Saying?)	Identifying the Issue (What's the Priority? - Choose from Dropdown List)	Customer Requirement (What's the Measurable Target?)
I shouldn't have to wait over 30 minutes for my order, especially if the food doesn't have to be cooked	Timeliness	Lunch order delivery in 20 minutes or less (entrees), 16 minutes or less for (salads, soups and sandwhiches)
Don't ignore me when I need something	Timeliness	Check in with customers in less than 5 minutes after the food order is delivered
Sometimes the soup isn't hot enough	Accuracy	Soup should be served at 155 - 160 degrees farenheit
Frequently you run out of my favorite lunch dishes	Choice	Food on the regular menu should be available 100% of the time

[Download Example] The team spent time speaking with customers on their way out or while they were waiting for their tables. They learned some new customer concerns and they found out that not all requirements are the same. Customers expect entrees to take longer than salads and soups. Good to know!

Roadside Assistance
How to Create a Voice of the Customer Translation Matrix

1. Determine the different customers or groups who receive the goods and services of the process.
2. For each group, list the comments, suggestions or feedback received regarding their process experience.
3. If there are many different requirements, use an Affinity Analysis to establish the natural groupings.

4. For each comment, list the underlying issue (e.g., "By the time I get my order it's almost time to get back to the office" has underlying issues of cycle time).
5. For each customer comment, determine what their requirement would be (e.g., for the above example, "meals delivered within 15 minutes of ordering").

Potholes and Detours Around Them

Potholes	Detours
Not clarifying which customer segment is being referenced in the comments	If multiple customer groups are represented, insert a row between them and label the groups.
Not capturing slightly different requirements within different customer segments	Go with the 80/20 rule and list the requirement that covers the majority.
Listing the requirement as a solution (e.g., for the above example, "hire more servers")	Check each requirement to ensure it is simply the measurable target such that there could be a number of potential solutions or ways to meet that requirement.
Generalizing Voice of the Customer	Don't generalize comments to the point of missing detail.

Sightseeing and Additional References

Templates:
- Voice of the Customer Translation Matrix
- Customer Value Checklist

Blogs:
- Do Government Agencies Have Customers or Hostages? Getting Your Customers to Rock n' Roll Over Your Products & Services

FROM THE TRAVEL KIT:
SIPOC

SIPOC

A SIPOC is a high-level view of a process.

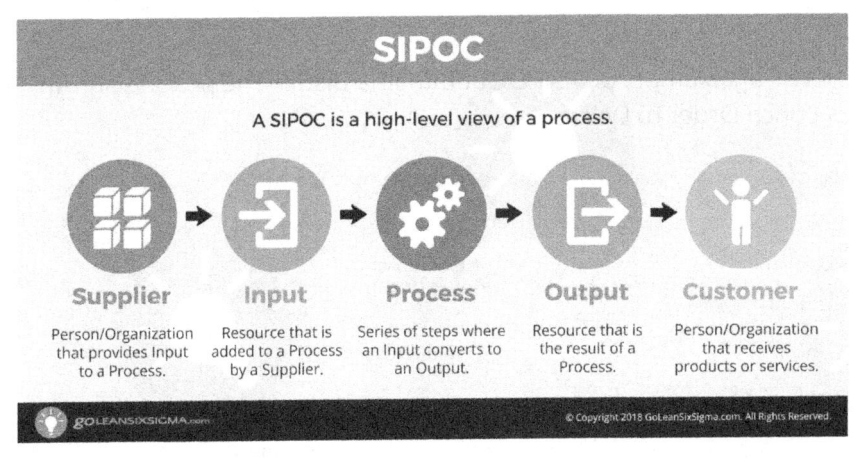

Supplier	Input	Process	Output	Customer
Person/Organization that provides Input to a Process.	Resource that is added to a Process by a Supplier.	Series of steps where an Input converts to an Output.	Resource that is the result of a Process.	Person/Organization that receives products or services.

© Copyright 2018 GoLeanSixSigma.com. All Rights Reserved.

What is a SIPOC?

A SIPOC is a high-level view of a process which stands for Suppliers, Inputs, Process, Outputs, and Customers. Every Process starts with Suppliers who provide Inputs to the Process which results in an Output that is delivered to Customers.

What Questions Will a SIPOC Answer?

- What is the process being addressed?
- What are the "start" and "stop" points (the scope) of the process?
- Who are the suppliers of this process?
- What are the inputs to this process?
- What are the 3 to 7 high-level steps of this process?
- What are the goods or services (output) that come out of this process?
- Who receives the goods or services that come out of this process (customer)?

- What are some potential areas of measurement for this process?

Example of a SIPOC

Here's an example of a SIPOC at Bahama Bistro. The process shown is Lunch Order to Delivery.

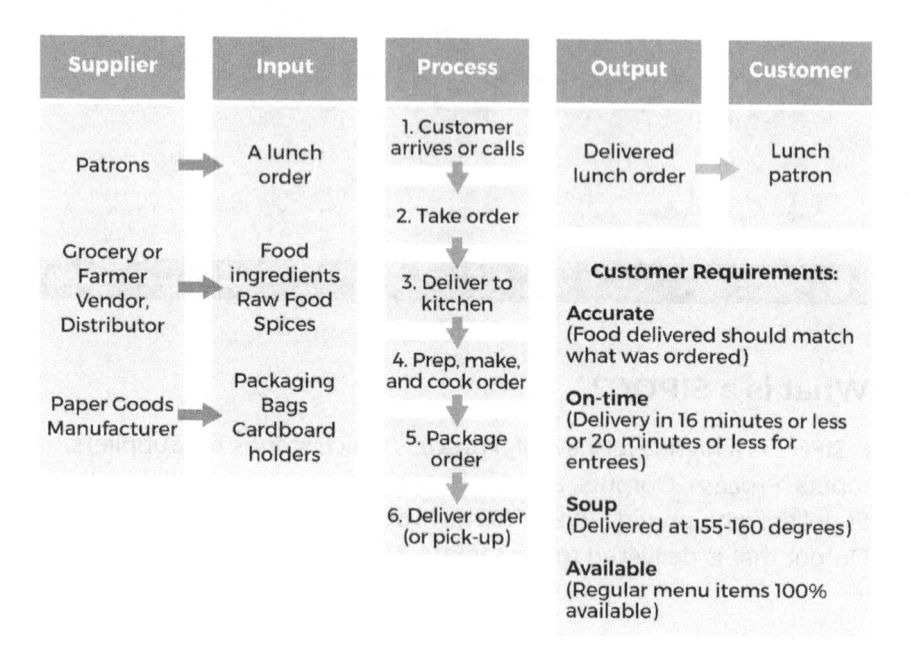

Supplier	Input	Process	Output	Customer
Patrons	A lunch order	1. Customer arrives or calls	Delivered lunch order	Lunch patron
Grocery or Farmer Vendor, Distributor	Food ingredients Raw Food Spices	2. Take order 3. Deliver to kitchen 4. Prep, make, and cook order	**Customer Requirements:** **Accurate** (Food delivered should match what was ordered)	
Paper Goods Manufacturer	Packaging Bags Cardboard holders	5. Package order 6. Deliver order (or pick-up)	**On-time** (Delivery in 16 minutes or less or 20 minutes or less for entrees) **Soup** (Delivered at 155-160 degrees) **Available** (Regular menu items 100% available)	

[Download Example] Seeing the process on one page helped the team understand the scope of the project. The lunch order would be a key input to track in the Measure Phase and they will most likely measure the cycle time of each high-level step.

Roadside Assistance
How to Create a SIPOC

1. Download the SIPOC template.
2. Determine the output of the process (e.g., completed applications, shipped product, hired employee, etc.) and place in the "Outputs" column.

3. List the recipients of the outputs in the "Customer" column (internal or external).
4. Determine the inputs to the process (requests, customer information, materials, etc.) and list in the "Inputs" Column
5. List the providers of each of the inputs in the "Suppliers" column.
6. List the 3 - 7 high-level steps in the "Process" column.
    a. There is a "Minimum Daily Requirement" of a verb and a noun (e.g., Enter information).
    b. Steps don't have to be linear.
    c. Don't include detail like rework loops.
    d. Assume detailed steps take place within the high-level steps.

Potholes and Detours Around Them

Potholes	Detours
Getting into the weeds of the process	Limit to 7 process steps maximum and use the Grateful Dead (or Snoop Dogg) Rule, "Stay as high as you can for as long as you can."
Experiencing difficulty figuring out who the customers are	Ask "who receives the goods and services of the process?" Be sure to understand the definition of a stakeholder. You might be confusing stakeholders with customers.
Listing dozens of potential inputs	Limit the inputs to what's important to the project — stay high level.
Listing the problem as the process	For example, "Scrap Creation" refers to a failure in a process, not the process itself.

Sightseeing and Additional References

Infographic:
- SIPOC Infographic

Blog:
- How to Use a SIPOC to Ensure Projects Are Scoped to Your Intended Customers

Webinar:
- 5 Ways a SIPOC Helps You Understand & Improve Your Process

Single Module:
- SIPOC Training

FROM THE TRAVEL KIT:
PROCESS (GEMBA) WALK

Process Walk

A Process Walk is an informational visit to a workspace that follows the "thing" going through the process.

1. Pick a Process to Walk
2. Create a High-Level Map
3. Identify People Who Work in the Process
4. Select Interviewees and Process Walkers
5. Create the Schedule and Walk the Process
6. Debrief Walk Observations

© Copyright 2018 GoLeanSixSigma.com. All Rights Reserved.

What is a Process (Gemba) Walk?

A Process (Gemba) Walk is an informational visit to where the work takes place by following the "thing" going through the process. It consists of a series of structured, on-site interviews with representative process participants with the goal of gaining a comprehensive understanding of the process.

Interviewees are invited to participate in walking the rest of the process with the other subject matter experts. Interviews focus on details such as lead time, process time, wait time, defect rates, root causes, barriers to flow and other information that can lead to targeted improvements.

What Questions Will a Process (Gemba) Walk Answer?

- How do we grasp the situation?
- What is the real process?
- How close is the current process to what we thought it was?
- Who does what throughout the whole process?
- What assumptions did we bust or confirm about the process?
- How long is the lead time?
- How much of the lead time is wait time vs. process time?
- What % of the time are things being done completely and accurately through the process?

Example of a Process Walk Interview Sheet

The Process Walk Interview Sheet is used for interviewing process participants. A Process Walk consists of several interviews conducted while walking the entire process. By the end of the Process Walk each interviewee has several completed Interview Sheets. Below is an example of a completed interview sheet.

Interviewer: Scott	Step #: 5	
Interviewee: Tracy	Step Name:	Don't forget to take pictures of the interviewees and the space.
Date: 15-Sep	Package Order	

Notes

1. How many people work on this step? How many people are shared resources and work elsewhere too? — # of staff / # of shared resources: 1 — She is a shared resource.
2. What % of the time do people have available to work on this step? — % of time available: 15%
3. How long from the time work is available to you until it is passed to the next step? — Lead time: 10 — There is some waiting for supplies
4. How long would it take to complete this activity if you could work on it without being interrupted or without waiting? — Work (touch) time:
5. What units received at this step are complete and accurate?
6. How many units are waiting to be worked on right now? Is that normal? How old is oldest job in the queue?
7. Do you have to set-up anything (equipment, etc.) before doing this step? If so, how long does that take?
8. What system is being used for this step? How do you track needed information (reports, spreadsheets, etc.)?
9. Batching: Is work "bundled" before moving to the next department? If so, how many units move to the next step at a time?
10. What issues or barriers to flow make this step painful or time-consuming? — Barriers to flow identified

Questions

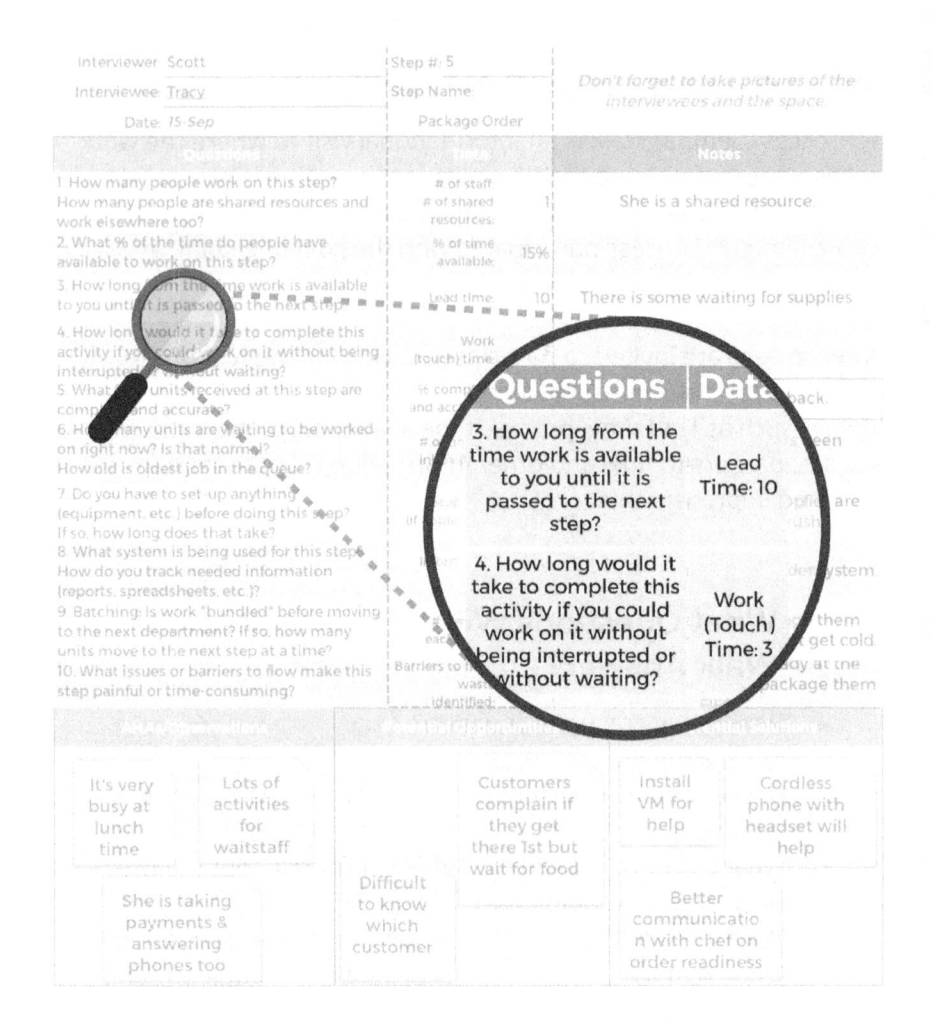

3. How long from the time work is available to you until it is passed to the next step? — **Lead Time: 10**

4. How long would it take to complete this activity if you could work on it without being interrupted or without waiting? — **Work (Touch) Time: 3**

It's very busy at lunch time	Lots of activities for waitstaff		Customers complain if they get there 1st but wait for food	Install VM for help	Cordless phone with headset will help
She is taking payments & answering phones too		Difficult to know which customer		Better communication with chef on order readiness	

[Download Example] The Bahama Bistro team discovered that Tracy was juggling a lot more tasks than they thought and they found some rework. The Process Walk is another great place to uncover waste. They put some of their improvement ideas into the "Solution Parking Lot" since they were still trying to understand the process.

Roadside Assistance
How to Create a Process (Gemba) Walk

1. Download the Process Walk Planning Checklist.
2. Build a SIPOC to Identify the high level steps of the process.

3. Use the SIPOC to list some of the process workers as potential Process Walk interviewees and participants.
4. Finalize the list of Process Walk participants.
5. Communicate the plan to stakeholders and participants (interviewees/walkers).
6. Create an interview schedule following the process order and allot 15-45 minutes for each interview.
7. Reserve a room for de-briefing between interviews and gather supplies including markers, clipboards, sticky notes, copies of interview sheets, etc.
8. Conduct a Process Walk Orientation for all participants prior to the Process Walk.

Potholes and Detours Around Them

Potholes	Detours
Splitting up to conduct the interviews and using a "divide and conquer" mentality	You need to stay together to build a shared understanding of the entire process.
Poor scheduling results in missing process participants	Be sure to invite *all* the interviewees to *walk* the process — not just to be interviewed. Ensure representation from every function or group that actually works within the process.
Making interviewees feel interrogated and intimidated	Enforce the ground rules throughout the whole Process Walk. If necessary, seek an unbiased facilitator.

Sightseeing and Additional References

Video:
- Process Walk: An Overview of What, Why and How

Templates:

- Process Walk Planning Checklist
- Process Walk Interview Sheet

Webinars:
- Process Walk Orientation for Participants
- Why Process Walks Are a Must

Single Modules:
- Process Walk Training
- Process Walk Facilitation Training

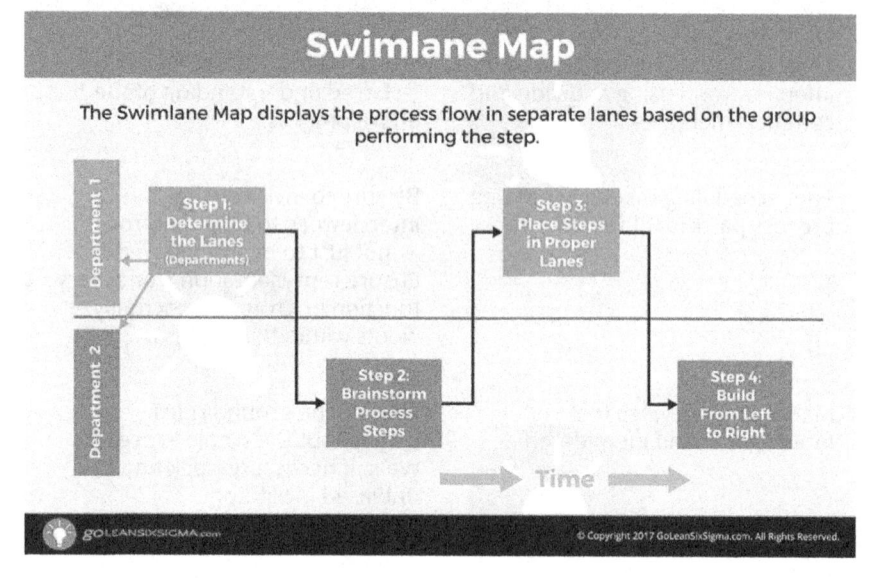

FROM THE TRAVEL KIT:
SWIMLANE MAP

Swimlane Map

The Swimlane Map displays the process flow in separate lanes based on the group performing the step.

Department 1
- Step 1: Determine the Lanes (Departments)
- Step 3: Place Steps in Proper Lanes

Department 2
- Step 2: Brainstorm Process Steps
- Step 4: Build From Left to Right

Time →

What is a Swimlane Map?

A Swimlane Map is a process map that separates a process into lanes that represent different functions, departments or individuals. The process map is called a "swimlane" because it resembles a pool with lanes identifying the different process groups.

What Questions Will a Swimlane Map Answer?

- What are the detailed process steps?
- Who works in this process?
- Who does which process steps?
- How many touches or handoffs does the "thing" or unit go through?
- Are there redundancies, bottlenecks or re-work loops in this process?
- When a decision needs to be made, what percentage of the time is it Yes vs. No?

Example of a Swimlane Map

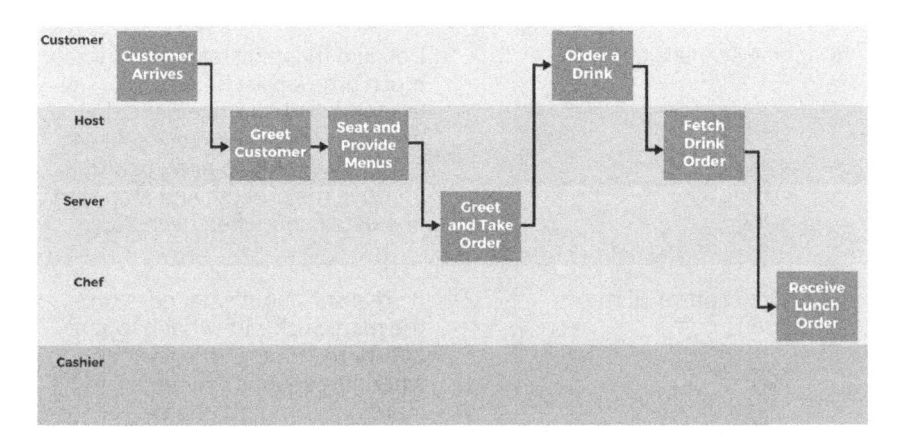

Customer	Customer Arrives			Order a Drink	
Host		Greet Customer	Seat and Provide Menus		Fetch Drink Order
Server				Greet and Take Order	
Chef					Receive Lunch Order
Cashier					

[Download Example] The team used sticky notes and found it fairly easy to build the map after conducting the Process Walk. They were surprised by the number of handoffs and planned to find out if they needed them all. They kept the map on the wall to keep it updated.

Roadside Assistance
How to Create a Swimlane Map

1. Identify the process and the mapping participants.

2. If possible, place background paper on a large wall space.
3. Label the lanes on the far left.
4. Decide on the level of detail needed by the team.
5. Talk through the process, and build the map with sticky notes representing each step.
6. Once the map is completed you can photograph it or transfer it into electronic form using the Swimlane Map template.

⚠️ Potholes and Detours Around Them

Potholes	Detours
Not involving the right people	Determine the level of detail needed and invite people that do that part of the process. Don't assume you know their process steps.
Mapping scope is too big	Detailed mapping takes time. If too much time lapses between mapping and improvement, the map becomes obsolete. Use it as soon as possible to analyze and improve the process and map with fine detail only when necessary.
Trying to capture all the exceptions	Be realistic about what goes on the map. Stick with what happens 80% of the time and make a note where exceptions take up an inordinate amount of time.
Performing parts of the process in different ways.	Sometimes it's worth mapping the different ways people do things in the interest of creating a standard process but this adds complexity. You may need to roll up to a higher level while mapping the larger process and then return to the detailed level when needed.
Mapping the Future State instead of the Current State	Process participants may jump to solutions and map the process as

it should be, instead of how it actually is. If you see this happening ask, "But, how does it happen today?"

Sightseeing and Additional References

Templates:
- Swimlane Map
- Swimlane Map (Bahama Bistro - Define Phase - Current State)
- Swimlane Map (Bahama Bistro - Analyze Phase)

Blog:
- 10 Successful Tips for Process Mapping

Single Module:
- Swimlane Map Training

FROM THE TRAVEL KIT:
VALUE STREAM MAP

Value Stream Map

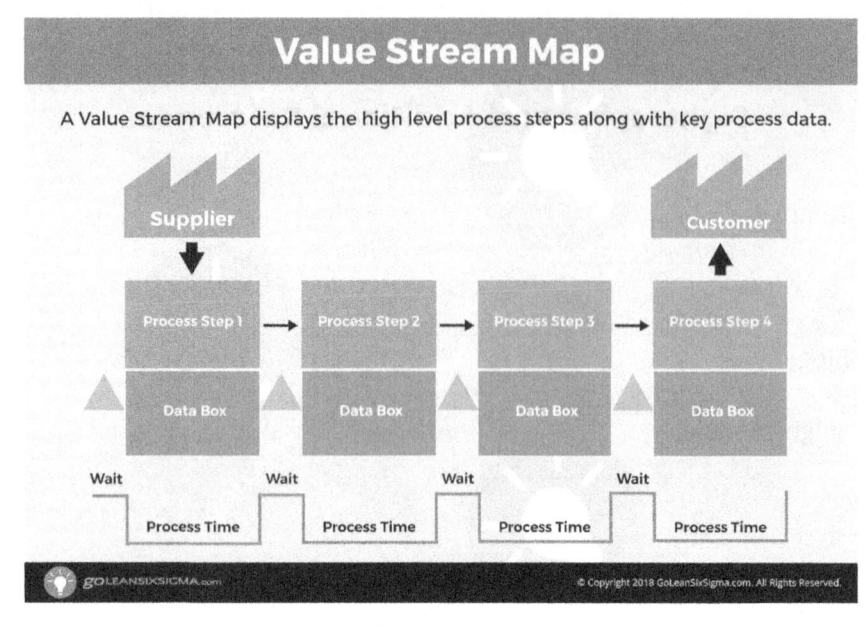

A Value Stream Map displays the high level process steps along with key process data.

[Diagram: Supplier → Process Step 1 → Process Step 2 → Process Step 3 → Process Step 4 → Customer, each with a Data Box below, and Wait / Process Time indicators underneath.]

GoLeanSixSigma.com — © Copyright 2018 GoLeanSixSigma.com. All Rights Reserved.

What is a Value Stream Map?

A Value Stream Map visually displays the flow of steps, delays and information required to deliver a product or service to the customer. Value Stream Mapping allows analysis of the Current State Map in terms of identifying barriers to flow and waste, calculating Total Lead Time and Process Time and understanding Work-In-Process, Changeover Time and Percent Complete & Accurate for each step.

What Questions Will a Value Stream Map Answer?

- What is the process across all departments and functions?
- What is the Total Lead Time, Process Time and Wait Time of this process?
- What are the barriers to flow in the process?
- How much Work-In-Process is there?

- Where is the waste?
- What percent of the time are things handed off as complete and accurate?
- Where are there opportunities to improve and streamline the process?
- Who is the customer?
- How fast does the process need to operate in order to meet customer demand?

Example of a Value Stream Map

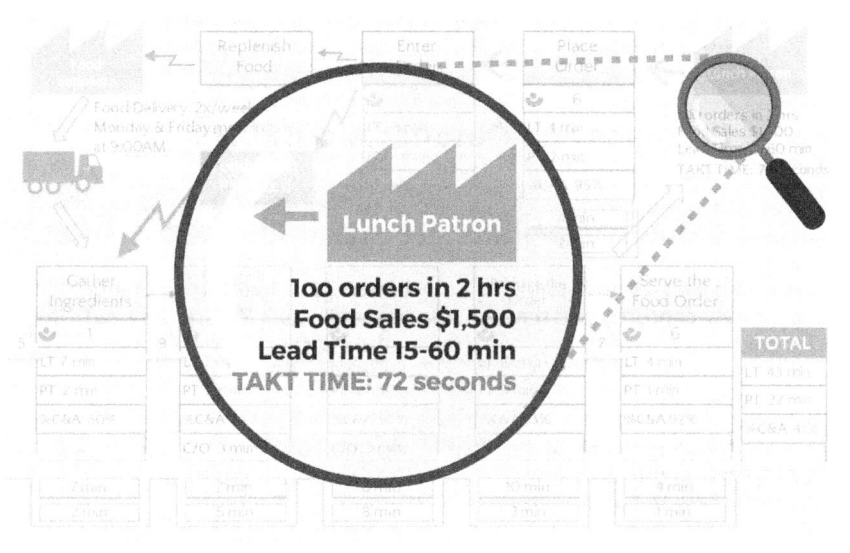

Lunch Patron
1oo orders in 2 hrs
Food Sales $1,500
Lead Time 15-60 min
TAKT TIME: 72 seconds

[Download Example] The team worked to determine time and accuracy data for each step. They were interested to find out that customers placed about 100 food orders every 2 hours and there seemed to be some quality issues. They planned to keep adding data to the map.

Roadside Assistance
How to Create a Value Stream Map

1. Download the Value Stream Map template.
2. Conduct a Process Walk with those that work in the process.

3. Use the interview sheets to gather process data during the walk.
4. Build the Value Stream Map with the collected process data.
5. Start with the customer and build the process steps.
6. Add the Work-In-Process or inventory between each process step if applicable.
7. Fill the data boxes with information from the interview sheets.
8. Build the timeline at the bottom of the map to calculate the Lead Time and Process Time for each step.
9. Add up the Total Lead Time and Process Time.
10. Analyze the Value Stream Map for improvement opportunities.

Potholes and Detours Around Them

Potholes	Detours
Worrying that it's impossible to accurately capture cycle time since it varies.	Don't get caught up in one-time exceptions. Capture the Lead Time and Process Time for what happens 80% of the time.
Taking too long to ask all the questions on the interview sheet to gather the Value Stream Map data	Instead of trying to gather *all* of the data just gather what's pertinent. Follow the recommendations for the manufacturing or transactional process data to collect. For example, changeover time is often not applicable in a non-manufacturing process.
Lacking the timeline at the bottom of the map	Be sure to map out the process, the information and the timeline at the bottom. These are the 3 critical components of a Value Stream Map.

Sightseeing and Additional References

Template:
- Value Stream Map

Single Module:
- Value Stream Map Training

FROM THE TRAVEL KIT:
A3

A3

An A3 is a one-page report on the background and current state of a project.

- Background
- Current Conditions
- Targets / Goals
- Analysis
- Proposed Countermeasures
- Implementation Plan
- Follow Up

GoLeanSixSigma.com © Copyright 2018 GoLeanSixSigma.com, All Rights Reserved.

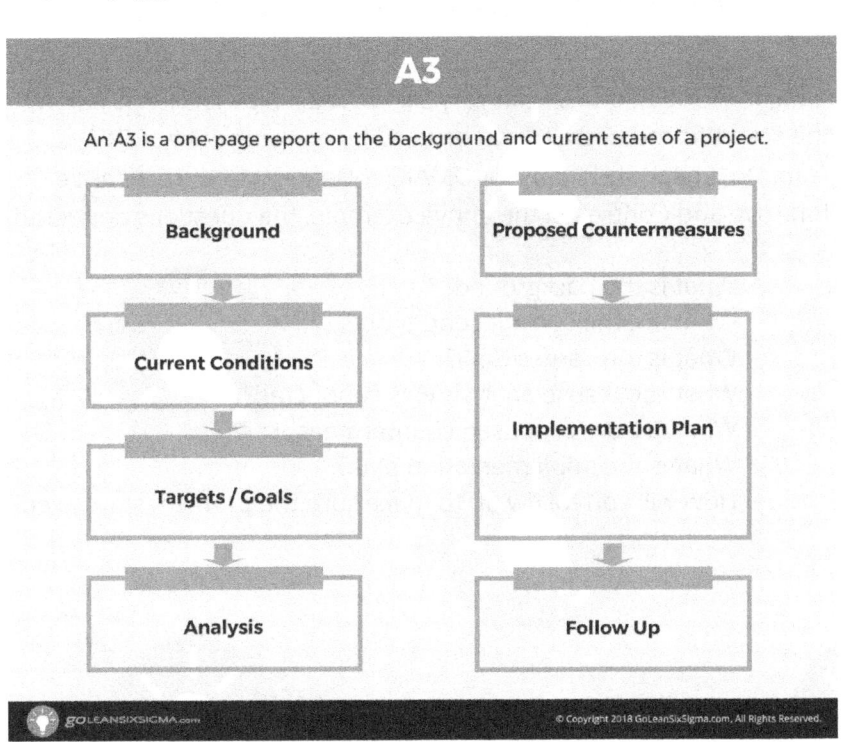

What is an A3?

On a literal level, A3 refers to a ledger size (11x17) piece of paper. But in the Lean Six Sigma world, it is a tool to help see the thinking behind the problem-solving. Don't mistake A3s as a document to be completed after the problem is solved. It's important to use the A3 while working through the problem.

The practice of using A3s forces project teams to focus their efforts. At the same time, A3s make it easier for a leader or coach to review a problem solver's work. A3s become valuable coaching tools since leaders can see and provide feedback on the problem solver's thought process.

What Questions Will an A3 Answer?

What is included on A3s can vary slightly. At a high level, A3s follow the scientific method and can be used by applying either PDCA — Plan, Do, Check and Adjust or DMAIC — Define, Measure, Analyze, Improve and Control. In the above example, the questions answered are:
- What is the background?
- What are the current conditions?
- What is the Target/Goal?
- What root cause analysis was conducted?
- What are the proposed countermeasures?
- What is the implementation plan?
- How will you follow up to make sure the problem stays fixed?

Example of an A3

Title: Bahama Bistro Lunch Order Delays

Name: Lunch Team
Date: January 14

Background
Good service is part of the Bahama Bistro Mission Statement. We can't afford to have dissatisfied customers - we'll lose them.

Current Conditions
It's currently taking 28 minutes on average to get lunch orders to customers. Customers are having trouble fitting this into their lunch hours.

Target(s) / Goal(s)
The goal is to deliver sandwiches and soups in 20 minutes or less and entrees in 30 minutes or less by May 10th

Analysis
Some of the root causes:
- Prep area is not set up efficiently causings lots of motion and restocking during the rush
- There are bottlenecks due to specialization of roles
- The lunch order form doesn't make it easy to call out special orders which leads to rework
- There is a lot of variation in the process based on the individual

Proposed Countermeasure(s)
Countermeasures proposed:
- 5S the Prep Area
- Conduct Cross-Training of all floor staff
- Redesign the order form to make special orders easy to see
- Institute Standard Work amongst all roles

Implementation Plan

Action Item (List Steps Required)	Responsible	Due Date
Meet with servers & cashiers to assess skills	Elisabeth	June 10
Fill out Cross-Training Matrix for each staff	Elisabeth	June 30
Develop time table for training sessions	Tracy	June 15
Arrange work schedule for mentoring	Tracy	June 17
Establish metrics and monitoring	Sean	June 19
Rollout training according to time table	Elisabeth	June 19
Meet with cashiers/servers to assess progress	Elisabeth	July 15
Adjust work schedule	Elisabeth	July 22
Determine need for continued monitoring	Tracy	July 24
Update Cross-Training Matrix	Elisabeth	July 24

Follow Up
Conduct 5S Audits and track scores on Run Chart
Use New Procedure Audit to check on adherence to Standard Work

[Download Example] The team decided to keep everyone updated throughout the project by filling out and distributing the A3. It was easy to do and it helped them all stay connected. The Bistro Owner looked forward to Fridays when he knew he'd get an updated A3.

Roadside Assistance
How to Create an A3

1. Download the A3 template.
2. Build the left side of the A3 first.

3. Socialize the problem with your team and others who work in the process.
4. Get agreement on the problem to be solved.
5. If possible, quantify the problem with data.
6. Analyze the problem for root causes.
7. Confirm root causes and work with your team to develop countermeasures.
8. Build an implementation plan for selected countermeasures.
9. Follow up after implementation is complete to ensure the problem stays fixed.

Potholes and Detours Around Them

Potholes	Detours
Waiting until the end of an improvement effort to complete an A3	Use the A3 to communicate throughout the project. Use it during the problem solving. Don't wait until after the improvement is completed.
Filling an A3 out alone (without others)	Use the A3 to collaborate and communicate with others including team members, key stakeholders and process workers.
Treating an A3 as documentation of the improvement — *after the fact*	Use the A3 as a learning tool during the effort. A3s can be great coaching tools for problem solvers. How an A3 is completed tells a coach a lot about the expertise of a problem solver.

Sightseeing and Additional References

Template:
- A3

Webinar:

- [How Leaders Use A3s to Coach Employees](#)

FROM THE TRAVEL KIT:
STAKEHOLDER ANALYSIS

Stakeholder Analysis

Stakeholder Analysis is the process of understanding who has a vested interest in a change effort and working with them to ensure success.

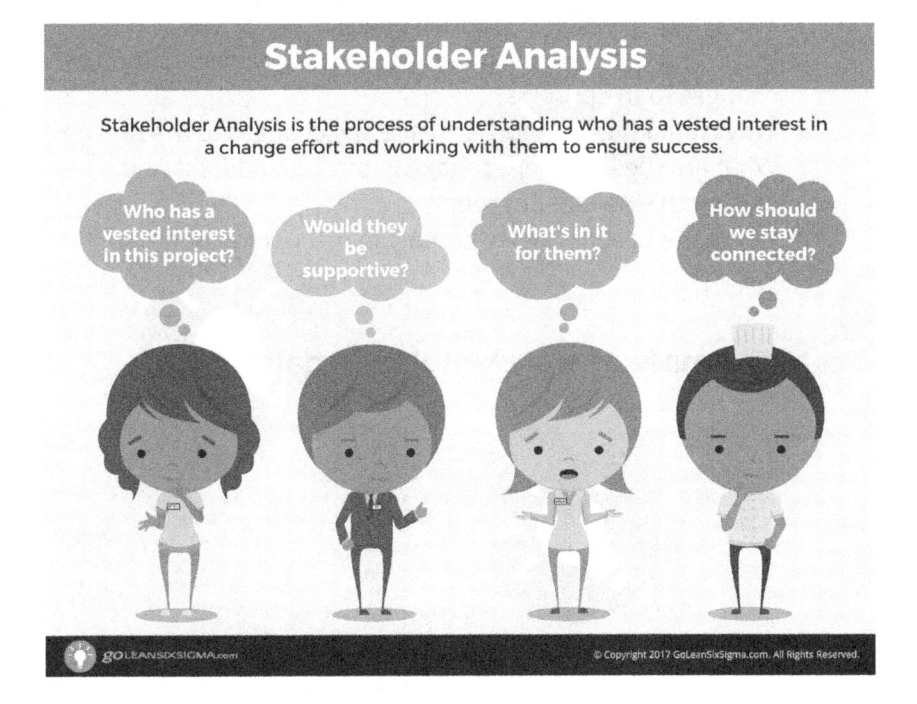

- Who has a vested interest in this project?
- Would they be supportive?
- What's in it for them?
- How should we stay connected?

goLEANSIXSIGMA.com © Copyright 2017 GoLeanSixSigma.com. All Rights Reserved.

What is Stakeholder Analysis?

Conducting Stakeholder Analysis enables you to outline who has a vested interest in how a process performs and what their concerns might be. Remember that stakeholders do not receive the product or service but they may be impacted if the process were changed. Sometimes they have the power to halt a project. Stakeholder Analysis helps you determine how and when to reach out and communicate with stakeholders to build trust and engagement, which is critical to a project's success.

What Questions Will Stakeholder Analysis Answer?

- Who is involved with this process?
- Who has a vested interest in how this process works?
- Who has the power to halt the project if they see fit?
- Who will be impacted by changes made to the process?
- Who could be a decision-maker in terms of granting permission to make process changes?
- Would each stakeholder support, resist or remain neutral to changes to the process?
- Why would they support or resist any changes to the process?
- What are the best steps to take in order to address and engage this person or group?
- Who's the best person to contact in this person or group?

Example of a Stakeholder Analysis

Stakeholder / Stakeholder Group	Impact Level	Level of Support	Reason for Resistance or Support	Action(s) to Address This Stakeholder Group	Contact
Manager	Decision Authority	Resister	Helped to design the current process - may not be aware	Invite to Team Meetings	Elisabeth
Prep Cooks	Impacts Outcome	Neutral	They are unaware of the problem	Interview for Process Walk	Sean
Servers	Will Be Affected	Supporter	They have heard customer complain and want to help	Interview for Process Walk	Tracy

[Download Example] The team realized that since the manager was part of the original process design, she might not understand or appreciate why there's a need to change it. They decided to invite her to a team meeting right away and keep her informed with the weekly A3 update.

Roadside Assistance
How to Create a Stakeholder Analysis

1. Brainstorm a list of people or groups who:
    a. Will be affected by any changes to the process in question
    b. Have the ability to impact the outcome of changing the process
    c. Have "decision-making authority" over any changes made to the process.
    d. Note: Use the "Relationship Map" as an aid to the brainstorming this list.
2. Determine each Stakeholder's relative impact level (Decision Authority, Impacts Outcome, Will Be Affected).
3. Determine each Stakeholder's position on changing this particular process.
    a. People and groups can be "Supporters", "Neutral" or "Resisters."
    b. Be sure to interview to determine their actual position and the reasons behind their positions.
4. List the reasons behind each Stakeholders' position on process change.
5. List actions to take with each stakeholder group
    a. If they are supporters, you may enlist them in engaging others.
    b. If they are resisters, you may work to understand their position in more detail.
    c. If they are neutral, you may engage them so they understand the bigger benefits of potential process change.
6. List the best team contact to reach out to the group.
7. Include any resulting communication efforts on the Communication Plan.

Potholes and Detours Around Them

Potholes	Detours
Missing a key Stakeholder group or individual because you aren't aware of them	Invite team members, sponsors and others to brainstorm the list of Stakeholders together.
Assuming a group is supportive, neutral or resistant when that isn't the case	Be sure to contact and interview members of each Stakeholder group to make sure you understand their true position on process change.
Putting the Stakeholder Analysis in a public space which offended the group labeled "resister"	Stakeholder Analysis is a private team document and should be treated as such.
Leaving out a Stakeholder because they are challenging	Remember, they still are a stakeholder. If you ignore them, you may not be able to get their support.

Sightseeing and Additional References

Blogs:
- You're Not the Boss of Me: 5 Ways to Influence Stakeholders
- 5 Effective Ways to Remember the Names of Project Stakeholders

Webinar:
- How to Manage Change With Negative Nancy

HELP WITH THE TRAVEL KIT:
Involve Other People

It might feel like getting things done yourself is more efficient, but be prepared for disappointment when nobody but you is excited about what you've done. Hopefully, by now you've identified some team members along with critical Stakeholders you can include in your efforts. People support what they help create.

Or said another way... before you hit the gas, make sure everyone is in the car with you. And don't forget to energize your team and stop for refreshments!

Define Phase: Summary

"Define" is the critical start point of the process improvement journey. Clarity up front means less wasted time down the road. Are you confident that you looked at the map, checked the traffic and adjusted your GPS?

Spend time with your Project Champion, team members and stakeholders to make sure you're all on the *same* trip and they'll appreciate you throughout the journey.

Define Phase Challenges

- Getting commitment from sponsors and team members
- Getting agreement on what problem to solve
- Not starting with a solution
- Involving the right people early enough in the process
- Spending the time needed on the Define Phase elements

Define Phase Best Practices

- Draft the Project Charter with the team to build ownership.
- Start the Goal Statement with "increase" or "decrease" and clearly identify the unit.
- Translate the Voice of the Customer into requirements as opposed to solutions.
- Publicize the Process Map and invite participants to verify the steps.

Journey Journaling

How are you doing? Car still working? Time to ask yourself a few questions:

- Is this still a good project? You can change your mind if you are already running into red flags with support or resources.
- Did you plan for a Process (Gemba) Walk? There's nothing better for building your understanding.
- What kind of progress have you made?
- What lessons did you learn?
- What would you do differently next time?

Now, it's time for some measurement!

Define Phase Journey

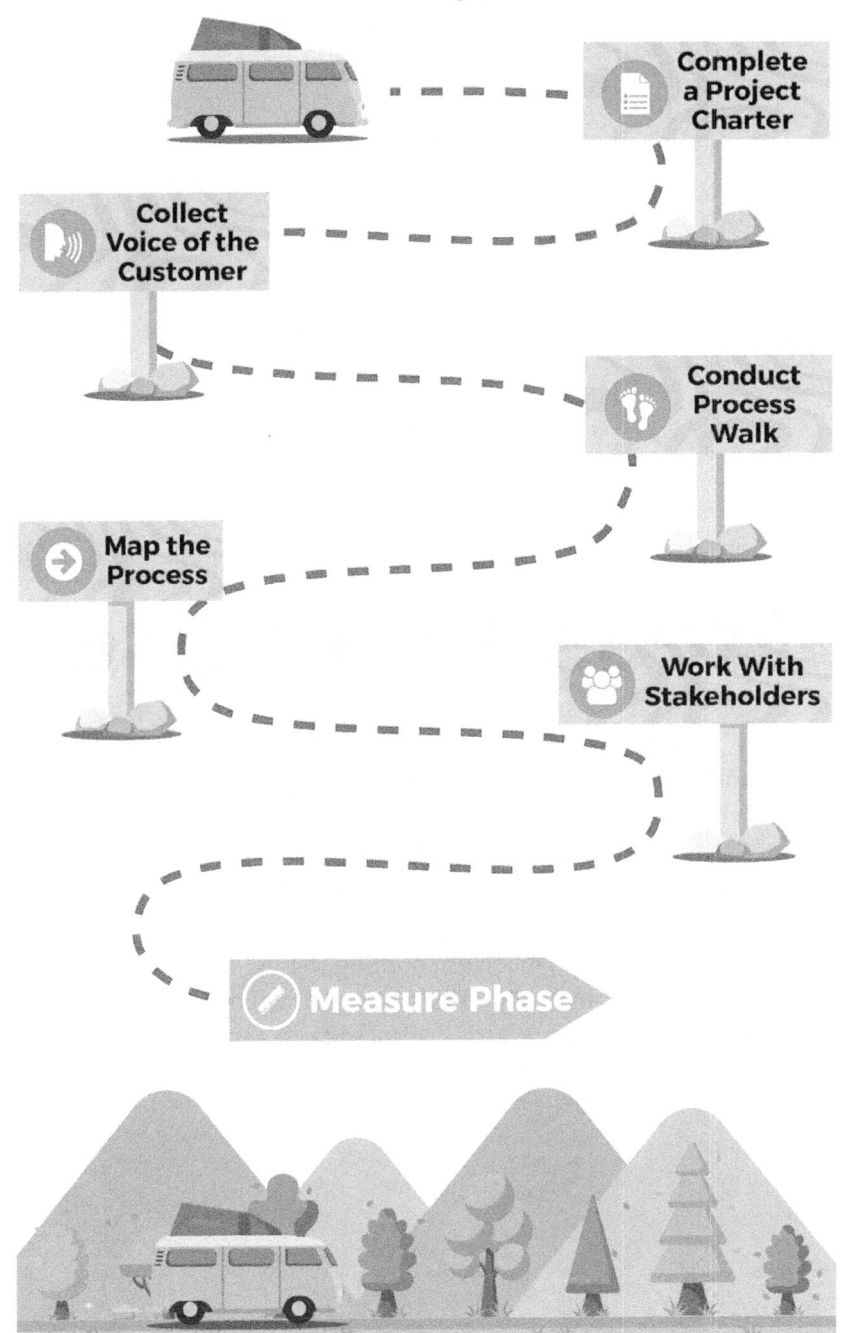

- Complete a Project Charter
- Collect Voice of the Customer
- Conduct Process Walk
- Map the Process
- Work With Stakeholders

Measure Phase

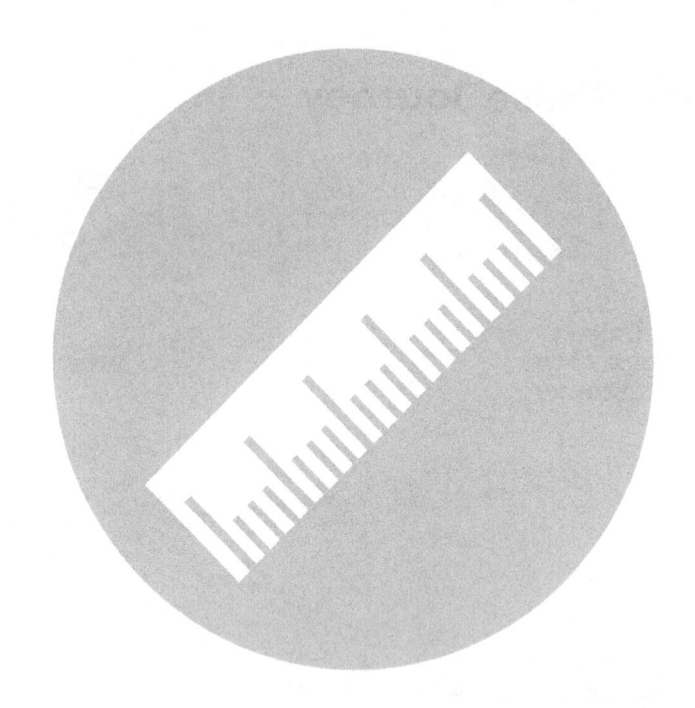

Measure Phase

Welcome Travellers! You are now moving into the Measure Phase of your road trip. Fasten your seatbelts as you may encounter some curves in the road. It would be great if there was a system full of perfect data and a convenient report with all the information you need, but that's probably not a realistic expectation.

Quantifying the problem involves counting things. That could mean you and your team physically writing things down on paper. Whatever it takes, getting data is critical to both assessing the status quo and getting clues to what's causing problems.

Pencils ready?

STEPS IN THE MEASURE PHASE

Select Measures

Figure out what you need to measure in order to baseline the process along with other measurements to help you understand the current state.

Plan for Data Collection

For each measure selected, create a plan so you and your team collect the *right* data in the *right* amounts with the *right* detail.

Collect Baseline Data

Follow your Data Collection Plan and collect enough data to understand the current state of the process.

MEASURE PHASE TRAVEL KIT — WHAT'S INSIDE:

Data Collection Plan
The Data Collection Plan is a roadmap detailing how to collect each piece of desired data.

Operational Definition
An Operational Definition is a detailed description that defines a measure to such a degree that everyone collects data the same way.

Takt Time
Takt Time (from the German "Tackzeit") is a formula that determines the pace or "drum beat" at which a finished product or service exits the process to keep up with customer demand.

Measures of Cycle Time
Measures of Cycle Time separate Total Lead Time into the time spent working on products and services versus the time the product or service is waiting to be worked on.

Check Sheet
A Check Sheet is a customized tally sheet that enables manual collection of the nature and frequency of process issues.

Baseline Measure
A Baseline Measure is data reflecting the "as is" state of the process.

FROM THE TRAVEL KIT:
Data Collection Plan

Data Collection Plan

The Data Collection Plan is a roadmap detailing how to collect each piece of desired data.

Measure Name
What would you call it?

Data Type
Is it discrete or continuous?

Operational Definition
What is the airtight description?

Stratification Factors
Will you slice data by who, what, where and when?

Sampling Notes
How much data will you collect?

Who and How
Who is responsible and what method will they use?

© Copyright 2018 GoLeanSixSigma.com. All Rights Reserved.

What is a Data Collection Plan?

A Data Collection Plan is a well-thought-out approach to collecting baseline data as well as data that can provide clues to root cause. The plan includes where to collect data, how to collect it, when to collect it and who will do the collecting. This plan is prepared for each measure and includes helpful details such as the operational definition of the measure as well as any sampling plans.

What Questions Will a Data Collection Plan Answer?

- What is the name of the measure?
- Is this a discrete or a continuous measure?
- How would you operationally define this measure such that everyone collected it the same way?

- Is there a calculation involved in the creation of the measure (e.g., Percentage).
- Will the measure be stratified by who, what, where or when?
- Is there data associated with the measure that might provide clues to root cause?
- How much data is being collected (e.g., 1 month, 2 months, a sample, etc.)?
- Who will actually conduct the data collection?
- Will they use a Check Sheet?
- Does the data reside in a system?
- Is the data included in a report?

Example of a Data Collection Plan

Measure Title	Data Type (Continuous or Discrete)	Operational Definition	Stratification Factors (by who / what / where / when)	Sampling Notes (Time Frame, etc.)	Who and How (Person Responsible and Method)
Order Lead Time	Minutes - Continuous	The amount of time (in minutes) it takes from the moment the patron places the order to the moment the order is delivered	By Time of Day By Server	Sample every 4th customer from 11 - 2 for the next 6 weeks starting 1/30	Host will check the time stamp on the security video
Incomplete Orders	Discrete	Any pick-up order missing the correct supplies including napkins, hot sauce, forks, or knives	None	Sampling all orders for 6 weeks to check for incomplete items	Cashier to fill in the check sheet for incomplete orders

[Download Example] Initially, the team was going to measure the time of a lunch order from when the server passed it to the kitchen, but that wouldn't take the customer into consideration. The server might get engaged in other tasks before the order made it to the kitchen. Luckily they could check the security tapes for time stamps!

Roadside Assistance
How to Create a Data Collection Plan

1. Download the Data Collection Plan template.
2. Start with the Project Y or main measure.
3. Assign the measure a name (Total Order Lead Time, % Application Defects, etc.).
4. List whether this is a discrete (e.g., defects) or continuous (e.g., cycle time) measure.
5. Operationally define the measure (e.g., What's considered defective? When does the cycle time start and stop?).
6. List any stratification factors (Lead time by employee, defects by defect type, lead time by district or defects by day of the week - who, what, where when).
7. Explain how much data is being collected (sample size or time frame).
8. List who will collect the data and how they'll do it.
9. If they'll be using a Check Sheet, attach it to the plan.
10. If it's within a system or based on a report, list both the system and the report(s).
11. Continue working through the plan for each measure to be used in the project.

Potholes and Detours Around Them

Potholes	Detours
Having different impressions of the measure	Review the Operational Definition with all data collectors and incorporate their feedback before collecting any data.
Data collectors not collecting data the same way	Test the data collection plan before launching the full scale data collection.

Not understanding why stratification factors are useful	Explain that they're a way to ensure you get associated data to help with clues to root cause.
Forgetting to include any stratification factors when collecting data	Remember up front to ask if there's a who, a what, a where or a when associated with the measure (applications by customer, etc.) - get clues to root cause along with the baseline data.
Not establishing responsibility for data collection	The team lead is ultimately accountable, but be sure to put individual names down if more than one person is collecting data. If "team" is listed, people may assume someone else will collect the data.
System missing some of the necessary data	Often data collection efforts result in a "hybrid" effort. An example would be "% Defective Applications." The total number of applications can be extracted from the system, but the team will need a separate Check Sheet to capture defective applications.

Sightseeing and Additional References

Templates:
- Data Collection Plan
- Operational Definition

Blogs:
- How to Control Your Blood Sugar Using Lean Six Sigma
- How to Lose Weight Using Lean Six Sigma
- What Does the Super Bowl Have to Learn From Lean Six Sigma?

Webinar:

- [How to Successfully Collect Process Data for Your Lean Six Sigma Project](#)

FROM THE TRAVEL KIT:
Operational Definition

Operational Definition

An Operational Definition is a detailed description that defines a measure to such a degree that everyone collects data the same way.

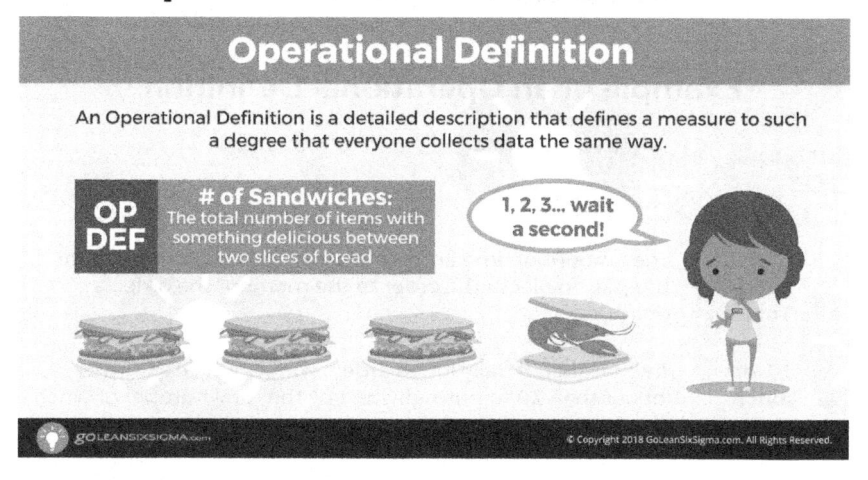

OP DEF — **# of Sandwiches:** The total number of items with something delicious between two slices of bread

1, 2, 3... wait a second!

goLEANSIXSIGMA.com © Copyright 2018 GoLeanSixSigma.com. All Rights Reserved.

What is an Operational Definition?

Operational Definitions describe the terms used within measures such as "accurate," "complete" or "defective" for time-based measures they define the start and stop points. These detailed descriptions of each measurement ensure that different data collectors interpret each measurement the same way. They are key to ensuring the integrity of measurement systems.

What Questions Will an Operational Definition Answer?

- What is the unit being measured?
- What is the granularity of the measure? (e.g., Days, Hours, Minutes, etc.)?
- If it's time-based, when does the clock start and stop?

- Is there a calculation involved in this measure (e.g., percentage or average)?
- Are there lists associated with this measure (e.g., what's "in" or what's "out")?
- If it's a physical characteristic, are there any photos for guides?
- What's the time frame for this measure (e.g., Daily, Weekly, etc.)?
- Have all the terms been defined?

Example of an Operational Definition

Measure	Operational Definition
Order Lead Time	The amount of time (in minutes) it takes from the moment the patron places the order to the moment the order is delivered.
% Late Lunch Orders	The number of daily lunch orders with Order Lead Times longer than 20 minutes divided by the total number of lunch orders for the day.

The team knew they had to define Order Lead Time, but they also wanted to measure the % of late orders. That was going to require a Check Sheet, but it shouldn't be too complicated for the servers to fill out. They decided a daily count would be the most useful.

Roadside Assistance
How to Create an Operational Definition

1. Choose a process measure to define.
2. Define the Project "Y" first - the main measure of the process being improved (e.g., Total Food Delivery Cycle Time).
3. Write a draft definition with team members.
4. Ask data collectors to review the definition and provide feedback.
5. Incorporate the feedback - critical step!
6. Develop job aids to assist in making the measurement (photos, checklists, etc.).

7. Ask people not involved in the project ("fresh eyes") to test the definition for potential misinterpretation.
8. Finalize the definition and train the data collectors.

Potholes and Detours Around Them

Potholes	Detours
Assuming everyone involved knows the measure and it doesn't require a detailed definition	Ask people to independently define the measure in their own words and check for variation (e.g., How would you define "business casual?").
Using the term "Percentage" but neglecting to clarify what's in the numerator and denominator	Include definitions for both the numerator (the defect or characteristic being tracked) and the denominator (the entire population being collected).
Leaving it unclear whether this is a daily, weekly or monthly measure	Specify the time frame in the definition.
Collecting hourly data but needing data in minutes	When determining the granularity of the measure, try to collect more specific data than you need at first.

Sightseeing and Additional References

Template:
- Operational Definition

Webinar:
- How to Successfully Collect Process Data for Your Lean Six Sigma Project

FROM THE TRAVEL KIT:
Takt Time

Takt Time

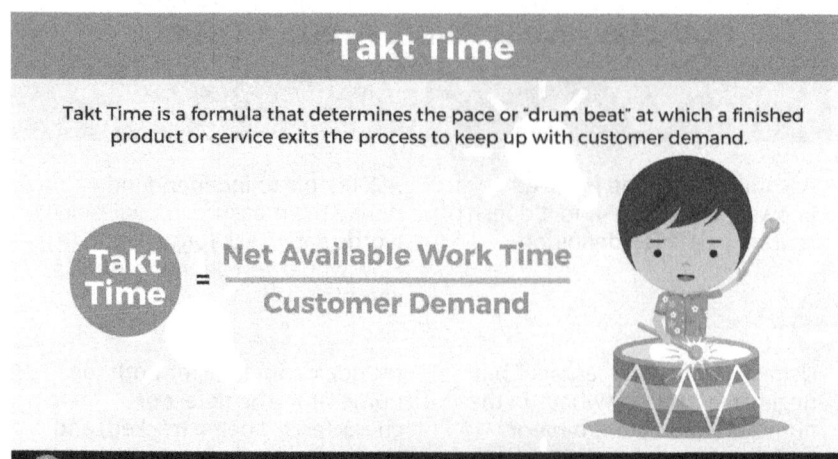

Takt Time is a formula that determines the pace or "drum beat" at which a finished product or service exits the process to keep up with customer demand.

$$\text{Takt Time} = \frac{\text{Net Available Work Time}}{\text{Customer Demand}}$$

What is Takt Time?

Takt is translated from the German word Taktzeit or "clock interval" meaning pace of production. Takt Time is the average time between the completion of one unit and the completion of the next. It's used to determine whether or not a process can keep up with customer demand. Takt Time is calculated by dividing the time available (minutes of work/day) by the customer demand (units required/day).

What Questions Will Takt Time Answer?

- How fast does the process need to operate in order to meet customer demand?
- What is the "drum beat" or pace at which the product or service must exit the process?

Example of Takt Time

> In order to figure out the customer demand rate, we divide the available work time by the customer demand.

> Okay, we serve dinner from 5 to 9pm so that's 240 minutes and we serve about 240 dinners on most nights.

> That's easy, 240/240 = 1. But, how can we cook a dinner in only 1 minute?

> No silly! It just means we have to have a dinner coming out of the kitchen every minute to keep up with demand. Lucky for us we've got more than one cook!

The Chef was helpful when trying to calculate Takt Time. He also had to remind the team that Takt Time was not the same as Process Time. Process Time is generally longer than Takt Time. The trick is to have the right number of people doing the right number of tasks at the right pace to meet customer demand.

Roadside Assistance
How to Create Takt Time

1. Determine the available work time.
2. Remove time for lunch, breaks, set up time, down time, parallel processes, etc.
3. Determine the number of units required by the customer within the available time.
4. Divide the available time (minutes of work/day) by the customer demand (units required/day) to calculate the Takt Time.

Potholes and Detours Around Them

Potholes	Detours
Confusing Takt Time with the time it takes to complete a step	Remember that it's the pace of work (1 completed every minute) as opposed to the time required to do the work (process time is 20 minutes).
Not removing lunch hours, break times, start-up time and shut-down time from the available work time	Use the actual available work time within a specified period of time.
Not adjusting Takt Time for parallel processes	Parallel processes may decrease your available work time and should be factored into the calculation.
Mixing up the numerator and the denominator	Be sure to put the available work time over the customer demand.

No Sightseeing Today

Time for a pit stop and a sandwich!

FROM THE TRAVEL KIT:
Measures of Cycle Time

Measures of Cycle Time

Measures of Cycle Time separate Total Lead Time into the time spent working on products and services versus the time spent waiting for them.

PROCESS TIME + WAIT TIME = LEAD TIME

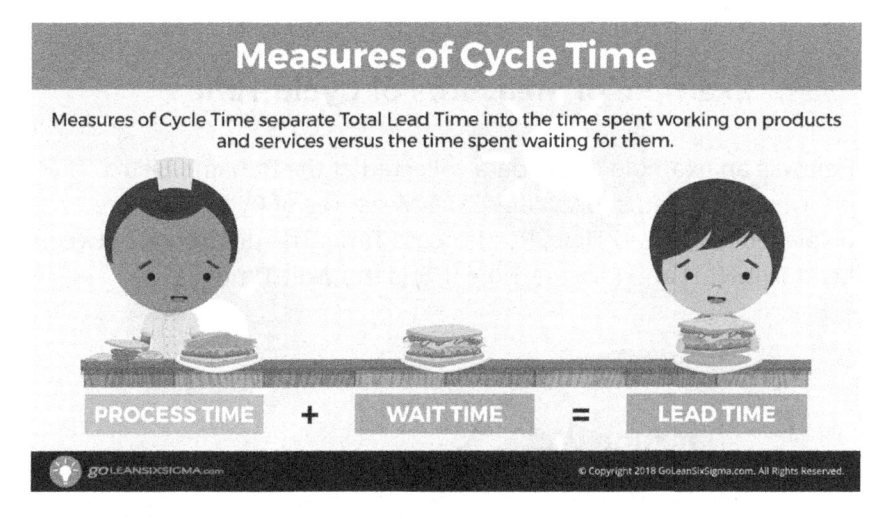

What are the Measures of Cycle Time?

Cycle Time comprises three separate categories of time:

- **Lead Time** measures the cycle time from the moment a customer places an order to the moment they receive the desired goods or services.
- **Process Time** measures the time a product is actually being worked on by a machine or by an employee. This is also known as Touch Time.
- **Wait Time** measures the time a unit or "thing" is sitting idle within a process. Waiting is often the most common of the 8 Wastes.

What Questions Will Measures of Cycle Time Answer?

- What is the total Lead Time of a process? (This is what customers experience.)

95

- What is the total Process Time (aka Touch Time) in this process?
- How much Wait Time exists in this process (Lead Time - Process Time)?

Example of Measures of Cycle Time

Below is an example of the data collected at the Bahama Bistro. The information in red shows where the Measures of Cycle Time are displayed. LT = Lead Time, PT= Process Time. The difference between Lead Time (LT) and Process Time (PT) is the Wait Time.

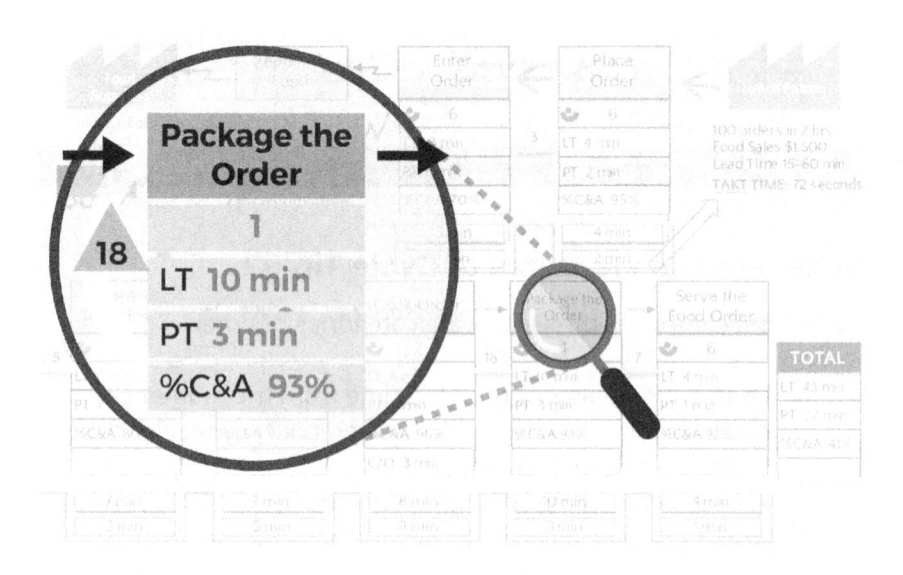

Package the Order

18

LT 10 min
PT 3 min
%C&A 93%

The team was surprised that almost half of the Lead Time was Wait Time, and there was a big bottleneck between cooking and serving. Order entry had a 30% error rate — that's a problem!

Roadside Assistance
How to Create Measures of Cycle Time

1. Download the Process Walk Interview Sheet and the Value Stream Map template.

2. Share the definitions of the Measures of Cycle Time prior to the Process Walk.
3. During the Process Walk ask interviewees for this information at each step of the process.
4. After the Process Walk use the Cycle Time information to build a current state Value Stream Map.

Potholes and Detours Around Them

Potholes	Detours
Not explaining or understanding the different definitions of Cycle Time	Ensure a solid understanding of each Cycle Time definition and why it's important to capture.
Focusing on the precision of the information rather than "in the ballpark" estimates	Much Cycle Time information is captured anecdotally from process walk interviewees. Spending too much time on data precision isn't as important as estimating how long things take.
Not capturing Cycle Time information	If the team suspects that Wait Time may be the culprit with process delays then that's important to capture.
Not understanding how to collect data.	Be sure to inspect how people are collecting data. Look at checksheets before data collection results in rework.

Sightseeing and Additional References

Templates:
- Value Stream Map
- Process Walk Interview Sheet

Single Module:
- Value Stream Map Training

FROM THE TRAVEL KIT:
Check Sheet

Check Sheet

A Check Sheet is a customized tally sheet that enables manual collection of the nature and frequency of process issues.

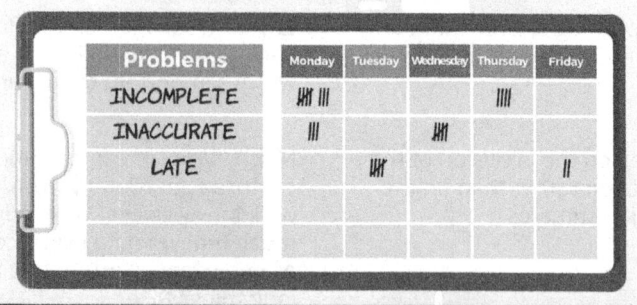

Problems	Monday	Tuesday	Wednesday	Thursday	Friday
INCOMPLETE	|||| |||		||||	
INACCURATE	|||		||||		
LATE		||||			||

What is a Check Sheet?

A Check Sheet is a simple tally sheet used to manually collect data on the frequency of an occurrence (e.g., the frequency of defects). Useful for all phases of DMAIC, Check Sheets are best used when the data can be collected by the same person or in the same location. It is particularly effective for identifying defect frequency, patterns of events and clues to the causes of defects.

What Questions Will a Check Sheet Answer?

- How will we collect data that doesn't currently exist in a system or database?
- What's a good way to manually tally information?
- What is a good way to collect information about defects or process failures as they happen?

- What's a good tool to provide to others so they can help with manual data collection?

Example of a Check Sheet

Date	Time	Food Order	Total Lead Time (min.)	Server	Prep Cook	Notes
2/2	1:04 PM	Conch Salad	22	Tracy	Scott	
2/2	1:20 PM	Flying Fish Waldorf Salad and Grouper Sandwich	25	Carlos	Julie	
2/3	12:20 PM	Beef Carpaccio and Conch Salad	30	Anna	John	New Prep Cook on the Conch Salad
2/4	1:15 PM	Conch Salad and Bahama Mama Smoothie	24	Darion	Cecilia	
2/4	1:20 PM	Flying Fish Waldorf Salad and Fish of the Day Sandwich	28	Tracy	Lynne	
2/4	1:33 PM	Flying Fish Waldorf Salad and Grouper Sandwich	45	Tracy	Scott	Had to comp the meal

[Download Example] The team decided that in order to understand what's causing the long lead times they needed to track which lunch items were late, who served them and who prepared them. With a little stratification, the team planned to get some insight on root causes while collecting baseline data.

Roadside Assistance
How to Create a Check Sheet

1. Download the Check Sheet template.
2. Find the measurement name and definition on the Data Collection Plan.
3. Include that information either at the top or attached to the Check Sheet.
4. Refer to the Data Collection Plan for any stratification factors.
5. Add a column to the Check Sheet template for each stratification factor.
6. Customize the template as needed (e.g., include a date column, include a column for notes, etc.).
7. Train each data collector on how to use the Check Sheet.
8. Have all data collectors conduct a test run to ensure they're all properly filling out the Check Sheet.
9. Incorporate feedback from users to refine the Check Sheet before full-fledged data collection.

Potholes and Detours Around Them

Potholes	Detours
Not filling out the Check Sheet correctly	Be sure to attach the operational definition(s) to the Check Sheet.
Not filling out all the columns of data required by the Check Sheet	Train each user before collecting data.
Not being prepared for unexpected defects and how to log them	Provide a "notes" column for data collectors to add observations if the data falls outside the expected range.
Not having enough background or descriptions on each defect	Be sure to include all useful stratification factors by adding a column for each to capture information related to the

	measure (by who, by what, by where and by when).
Not filling out the Check Sheet because it takes too long	Make it easy for data collectors by requiring the most simple form of information such as hash or check marks.
Logging similar types of defects but listing them in slightly different ways	Predefine as many potential defects as possible and provide that list for users.
Writing down "other" in spite of the existence of a pre-made list of defect types	Be sure to test the Check Sheet before full implementation to find out all the potential defects types from the data collectors first.

Sightseeing and Additional References

Template:
- Check Sheet

Webinar:
- How to Successfully Collect Process Data for Your Lean Six Sigma Project

FROM THE TRAVEL KIT:
Baseline Measure

Baseline Measure

A Baseline Measure is data reflecting the "as is" state of a process.

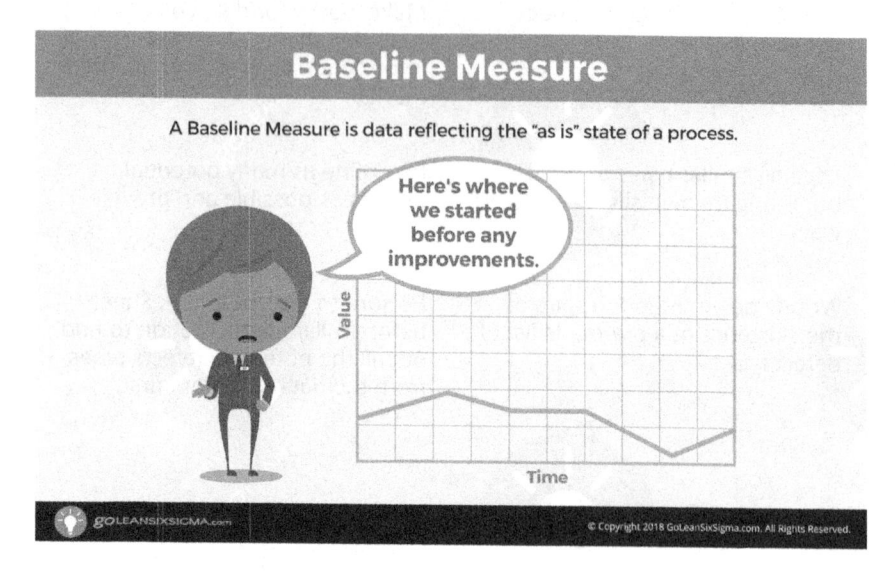

Here's where we started before any improvements.

What is a Baseline Measure?

A Baseline Measure results from data collected to establish the initial capability of a process to meet customer expectations. By collecting a baseline prior to making any changes to the process, it is possible to determine if solutions implemented later on have had the desired impact. It's also a way to check if the problem is as bad or worse than expected. If it's not that bad, the team my switch to tackling a new process problem.

What Questions Will the Baseline Measure Answer?

- What is the current capability of the process being improved?
- How does the process capability compare to customer expectations?
- What's the gap between the current process capability and the desired state?

Example of a Baseline Measure

In this Bahama Bistro example, the baseline measure of the Project Y would be the existing average Order Lead Time. This Run Chart (covered in Analyze) and Histogram (covered in Analyze) both display the current baseline performance of Order Lead Time. It's important to see the data over time to get a sense of the trend with process performance.

Baseline Lunch Order Lead Time - Run Chart

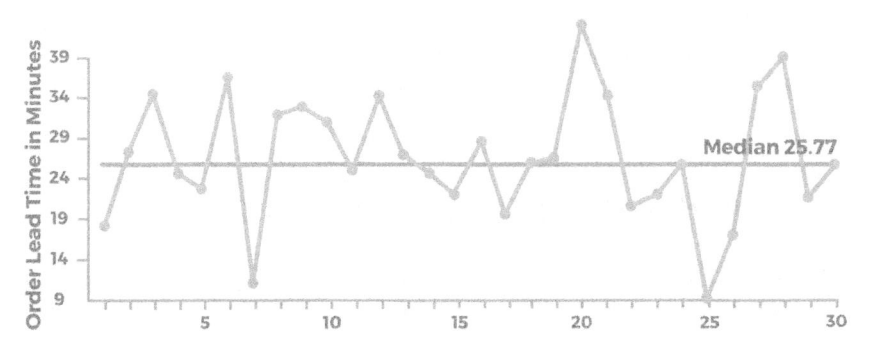

Median 25.77

Baseline Lunch Order Lead Time - Histogram

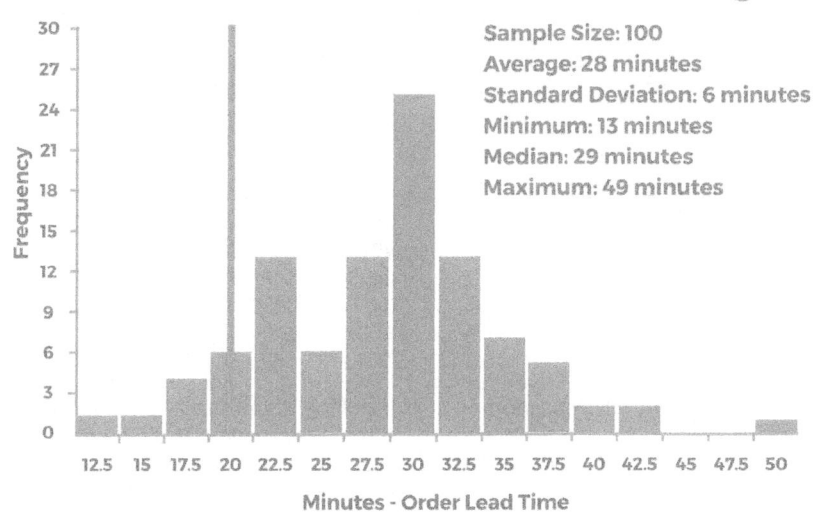

Sample Size: 100
Average: 28 minutes
Standard Deviation: 6 minutes
Minimum: 13 minutes
Median: 29 minutes
Maximum: 49 minutes

The team knew the lunch time was too long, so they used the most recent data for the Run Chart. When they used a bigger sample of lunch orders to create the Histogram they realized the problem was worse than they thought. Seeing how many orders were past the 20 minutes expected by customers meant Order Lead Time was definitely a problem to be fixed!

Roadside Assistance
How to Create a Baseline Measure

1. Refer to instructions for creating a Run Chart and or a Histogram (SigmaXL instructions, Minitab instructions).
2. Gather the most recent baseline data.
3. Chart your Project Y (Measure referenced in the Project Goal).

Potholes and Detours Around Them

Potholes	Detours
Not being able to measure or quantify the Project Y	Be sure to select a DMAIC project where progress will be measurable and quantifiable.
Not being able to access any system for existing baseline data	Use the Data Collection Plan and Check Sheets to manually collect baseline data.
Waiting until all the data is collected before moving on to the Analyze Phase	By studying the data as it comes in, you get a head start on Analyze, and might discover something that causes a change in how you collect data. It's best to find that early, not at the end.
Missing potential stratification factors.	If pulling data from a database, it's often easy to include all the fields that are potentially useful. It might provide useful root cause

information and it's easy to discard.

Sightseeing and Additional References

Templates:
- Data Collection Plan
- Check Sheet

Webinars:
- How to Successfully Collect Process Data for Your Lean Six Sigma Project
- 5 Ways to Create Charts & Graphs to Highlight Your Work

Measure Phase: Summary

The Measure phase is the workhorse of improvement projects. Without enough good data, it's hard to know how well a process is truly functioning and where to target analysis and then improvements.

It's like figuring out exactly how much gas you have before heading down the road. Take the time here to ensure your decisions are fact-based and you won't get stranded on the side of the road! Time to take that data and see what the Analyze Phase has in store.

Measure Phase Challenges

- Getting support and coordination from others in order to capture data
- Planning data collection to minimize work and disruption
- Capturing data that addresses your information needs
- Becoming overwhelmed with data when only some will be helpful

- Translating what you want to know into something observable and unambiguous
- Determining measures that can be continuously captured in order to manage the future process

Measure Phase Best Practices

- Choose just the measures you need — don't collect the kitchen sink.
- Make sure everyone knows what and how to measure — never assume.
- Stratify early — unit by time of day, unit by processor, unit by area, etc.
- Let stakeholders know what and why you're measuring — communicate often.

Journey Journaling

How are you doing? Are you running out of gas? Time to ask yourself a few questions:
- Is the process as bad as you thought? Worse? Better?
- Do you want to collect more data?
- What kind of progress have you made?
- What lessons did you learn?
- What would you do differently next time?

Measure Phase Journey

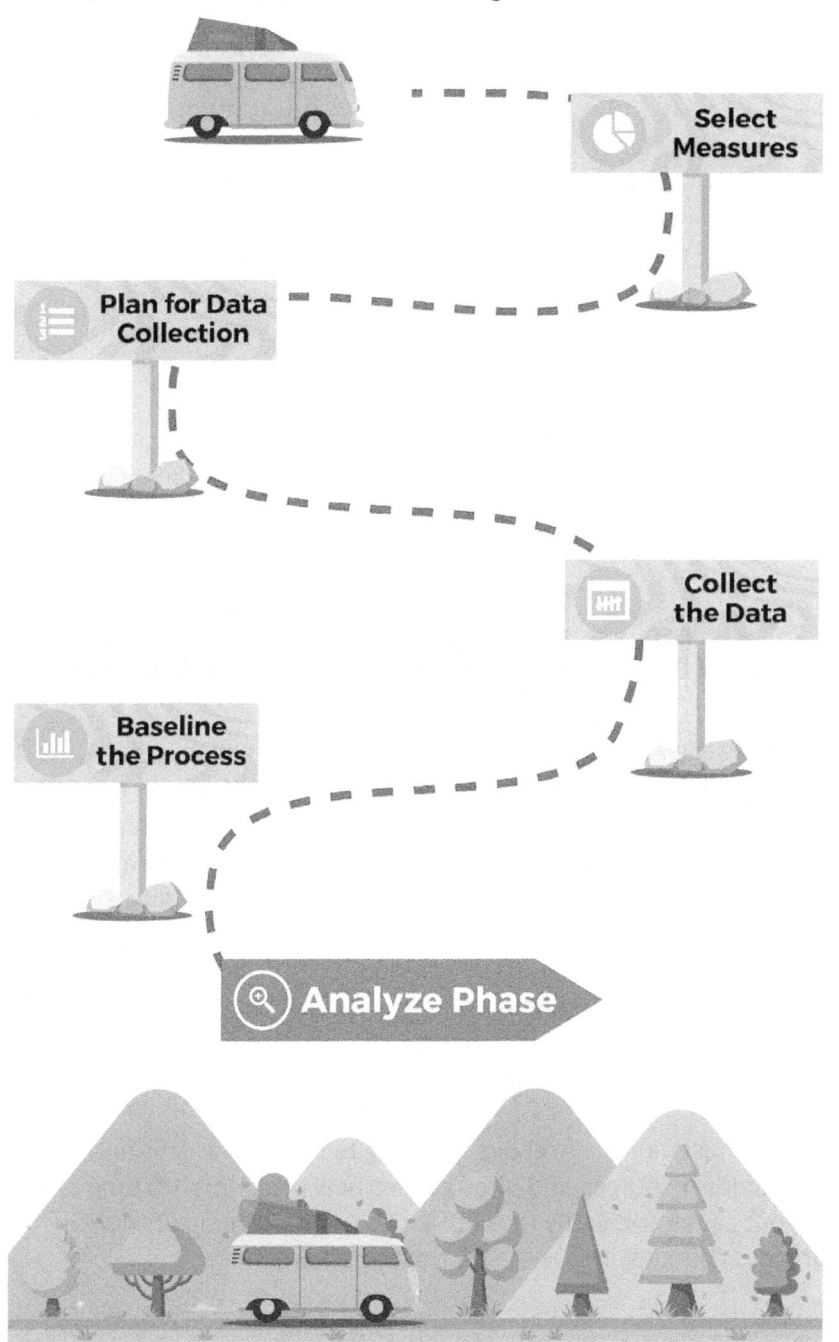

- Select Measures
- Plan for Data Collection
- Collect the Data
- Baseline the Process

Analyze Phase

Analyze Phase

Reaching the Analyze Phase means the team is making great progress — but beware! Some travellers are in such a rush to get to the Improve Phase they look for a detour to bypass this step altogether. If you haven't been here before, it can feel like an uphill journey. But this part of the trip can be the *most* rewarding. Don't let your team take a shortcut!

If the team jumps to solution the result is "solutions" that don't resolve the problem. That's like hearing a knocking sound in the engine and immediately replacing the carburetor!

As with misguided car repairs, jumping to solution wastes time, consumes resources and often causes new problems. It's time to dig to root cause and verify those theories before coming up with process changes. This is the crux of improvement!

STEPS IN THE ANALYZE PHASE

Conduct Process Analysis

Analyze the process maps and look for rework, redundancies, bottlenecks and other issues that get in the way of the process flow.

Conduct Data Analysis

Create charts and graphs of the data collected in the Measure Phase to look for trends, shifts or patterns that help with understanding the different factors inhibiting the process performance.

Brainstorm Root Causes

Gather the wisdom of team members, stakeholders and process participants to collectively drill to root cause.

Develop Root Cause Hypotheses

Determine which root causes to pursue and clarify each theory.

Validate Root Cause Hypotheses

Use data, observation, testing or the most logical method to confirm or rule out each root cause theory.

ANALYZE PHASE TRAVEL KIT — WHAT'S INSIDE:

Value-Added Flow Analysis
The Value-Added Flow Analysis assesses which steps add value in the eyes of the customer and where time and effort are wasted in the process.

Pareto Chart
A Pareto Chart is a bar chart that displays the most significant types of defect occurrences in descending order.

Histogram
Histograms show the distribution of values in a data set while highlighting the center, spread and shape of the data.

Run Chart
A Run Chart is a time series plot that displays shifts and trends in data over time.

Box Plot
A Box Plot compares the distribution of different data sets by dividing them into fourths or "quartiles."

Scatter Plot
A Scatter Plot displays whether changes in an independent variable correlate to changes in a dependent variable.

Fishbone Diagram
A Fishbone Diagram is a structured brainstorming tool using categories to explore root causes for an undesirable effect.

5 Whys
The 5 Whys is a simple analysis technique that moves past symptoms by asking "why" until reaching the true root cause of an issue.

Root Cause Hypothesis Statement

A Hypothesis Statement is an educated guess about the suspected cause (or causes) of defects in a process.

FROM THE TRAVEL KIT:
Value-Added Flow Analysis

Value-Added Flow Analysis

The Value-Added Flow Analysis assesses which steps add value in the eyes of the customer and where time and effort are wasted in the process.

Value-Added Step	Non-Value-Added Step	Non-Value-Added but Required Step
Time Spent on the Customer	Wasted Time	Unavoidable Wasted Time

What is a Value-Added Flow Analysis?

Value-Added Flow Analysis combines two powerful tools into one. The Value Analysis differentiates steps that add value in the eyes of the customer from those that do not, and Flow Analysis calculates the time spent on each step. This makes clear the time and effort being spent on non-value-adding activities, which represent pure costs to your business — much of which can be targeted and eliminated! This sets the stage for reducing waste and streamlining the process.

What Questions Will a Value-Added Flow Analysis Answer?

- Which process steps do/do not add value in the eyes of the customer?
- Which process steps don't add value but are required by the business or a governing body?
- How much *time* is spent on activities the customer is willing to pay for?
- How much *time* is spent on non-value-adding activities?
- How much *time* does the "thing" (process unit) remain idle?
- What's the cost of doing business in this process?

Example of a Value-Added Flow Analysis

Name: Tracy
Date: March 10
Process Name: Lunch Order to Delivery
Time Measured In: (Minutes) Hours Days

Process Step	Step Label (VA, NVA, NVA-r)	Value Added Time	NVA & NVA-r Required Work Time	NVA - Wait Time
Walk the customer order to the kitchen	NVA		2	
Check if it's readable	NVA		2	
If not readable, bring back to the waitress	NVA		2	
Ask the waitress to clarify the order	NVA		2	
Walk the customer order back to the kitchen	NVA		2	
Prep cook passes the order to the chef	NVA		2	
Chef assesses the order	NVA-r		2	
Ingredients assembled	VA	2		
Order cooked and prepared	VA	7		
Order plated	NVA-r		1	
Order placed on the warmer/staging	NVA			1
Order waits for pickup	NVA			10
Waitress picks up order	NVA			2
Customer receives order	VA	1		

	Time	% of Total
Total Value-Added Work Time	10	26.32%
Total Non-Value-Added or NVA-r Work Time	15	39.47%
NVA - Wait Time	13	34.21%
Total Cycle Time	38	100.00%

[Download Example] The team discovered that over a third of the total Total Lead Time was Wait Time. They figured out there was some opportunity to reduce that, but there might be some other opportunities with all the Non-Value-Added-But-Required steps. They'd get to that after they got through studying the Wait Time.

Roadside Assistance
How to Create a Value-Added Flow Analysis

1. Download the Value-Added Flow Analysis template.
2. List each process step in order of the process being analyzed
3. If there are times a unit is waiting, list those as separate steps
4. Label each step Value Adding (VA) if all of the following criteria are true:
    a. It changes the item or service toward completion (not simply "reviewed," etc.).
    b. The customer cares about the step or is willing to pay for it.
    c. It's done right the first time (this is not an inspection & rework step).
5. Label the step Non-Value Adding but Required (NVA-r) if it is either a business or regulatory requirement and label it Non-Value Adding (NVA) if not.
6. Determine the time it takes to perform each step and enter the timing in the appropriate column based on whether you labeled it VA, NVA or NVA-r.
7. Check the totals for opportunities to remove wait time from the process.

Potholes and Detours Around Them

Potholes	Detours
Mistakenly assuming that a person is Non-Value-Added	Be clear that it's the work that is non-value-added. People are valuable and you don't want to waste their talent on non-value-added steps.
Not capturing the true wait time within the process	Separate the time a unit is being worked and the time a unit remains idle into separate steps to properly capture wait times.

Defensiveness about having the work people do labeled "Non-Value Added"	If there's a dispute, work toward agreement on the steps that are Value-Added (sometimes that's easier). Then focus on opportunities to minimize, simplify or eliminate regardless!
Not understanding specifically where time is wasted in the process	Be sure to use a detailed as opposed to a high-level process map.

Sightseeing and Additional References

Template:
- Value-Added Flow Analysis

FROM THE TRAVEL KIT:
Pareto Chart

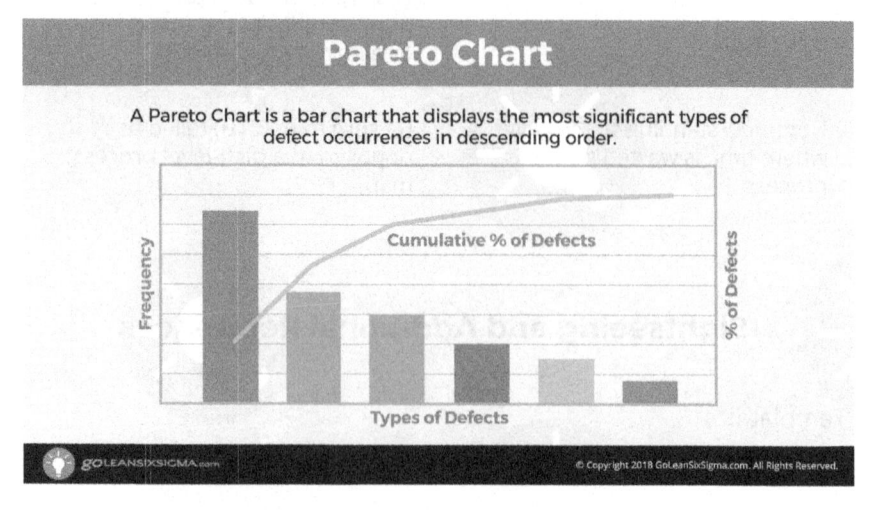

> **Pareto Chart**
>
> A Pareto Chart is a bar chart that displays the most significant types of defect occurrences in descending order.
>
> *Frequency* | Cumulative % of Defects | *% of Defects*
>
> Types of Defects
>
> goLEANSIXSIGMA.com © Copyright 2018 GoLeanSixSigma.com. All Rights Reserved.

What is a Pareto Chart?

A Pareto Chart is a Bar Chart of discrete data that displays the most significant categories of defects in descending order. The chart was named after the Italian economist, Vilfredo Pareto, who discovered the "80/20 Rule." The Pareto Chart uses the 80/20 Rule to narrow the focus of process improvement to the 20% of defect categories causing 80% of the process issues.

Pareto Charts display both frequency of occurrences (bar graph) and cumulative percent of occurrences (line graph) on a single chart. The left Y-Axis shows frequency of occurrences, while the right Y-Axis shows the total percentage.

What Questions Will a Pareto Chart Answer?

- Does the data exhibit the 80/20 rule?
- What are the most frequently occurring categories of defects?

- What percentage of the total data set does each category represent?
- What is the biggest issue?
- What's a good place to focus the improvement efforts?

Example of a Pareto Chart

All Food Sales

Types of Orders	Frequency	% of Orders
Salads	22	22%
Combinations	20	42%
Sandwiches	18	60%
Entrees	17	77%
Soups	13	90%
Desserts	10	100%

They didn't see the 80/20 Rule in effect, but they did see that the most popular lunch items were salads, although combination orders and sandwiches were close seconds. They decided to start measuring the prep times of each to see if they contributed to long lunch order lead times.

Roadside Assistance
How to Create a Pareto Chart

1. Determine the different categories of defects within the process.
2. Use Check Sheets to collect defect data for each category.

3. Enter the totals for each category in a spreadsheet such as Excel.
4. Use your graphical package of choice to create a Pareto Chart.
5. See links below to use SigmaXL or Minitab to create a Pareto Chart.

Potholes and Detours Around Them

Potholes	Detours
Not finding a Pareto Effect (80/20 rule) in the data being analyzed	That is called a "Flat-tato" (no, just kidding). The 80/20 Rule isn't always present in your data but you can still benefit from focusing on the tallest bars which represent the biggest sources of problems.
Mistaking the Pareto Chart for a Bar Chart	Pareto Charts display the categories from highest to lowest bar. Bar charts do not. Be sure you're creating a Pareto Chart and not just a bar chart. Don't forget the cumulative percent line.
Using a Pie Chart instead of a Pareto Chart	Pie Charts are OK if you have fewer than 5 categories, but Pie Charts don't create cumulative percent totals either. Pareto Charts make it easier to focus on the source of the greatest issues.

Sightseeing and Additional References

Templates:

- How to Create a Histogram in SigmaXL
- How to Create a Histogram in Minitab

Webinars:

- How to Successfully Collect Process Data for Your Lean Six Sigma Project
- 5 Ways to Create Charts & Graphs to Highlight Your Work

FROM THE TRAVEL KIT:
Histogram

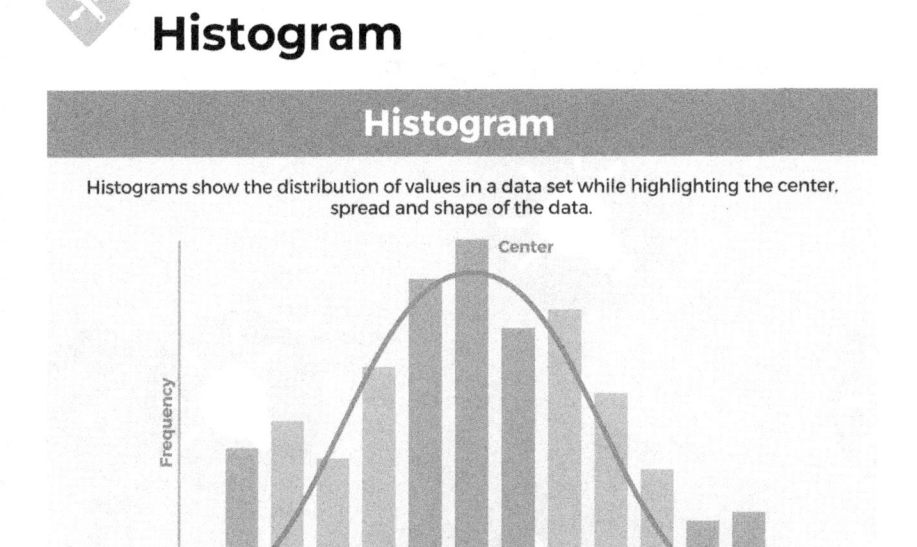

Histogram

Histograms show the distribution of values in a data set while highlighting the center, spread and shape of the data.

Frequency / *Center* / *Spread*

What is a Histogram?

Histograms, also known as Frequency Plots, are visual displays of how much variation exists in a process. They highlight the center of the data measured as the mean, median and mode. They highlight the distribution of the data measured as the range and standard deviation and the shape of a Histogram indicates whether the distribution is normal, bimodal or skewed.

What Questions Will a Histogram Answer?

- What is the center of my data set?
- How much spread is in my data set?
- What is the shape of my data set?
- How is the process performing compared to what customers want?

Example of a Histogram

Time to Prepare Meals

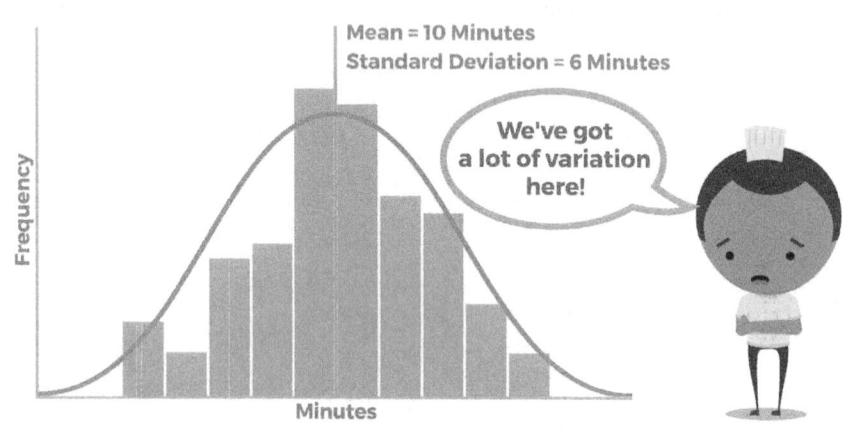

Mean = 10 Minutes
Standard Deviation = 6 Minutes

We've got a lot of variation here!

Frequency / Minutes

The team looked at the overall prep times and realized they had a lot of variation. They needed to stratify the data into the different food orders to understand where the variation was coming from. Time to try out some other forms of data display.

Roadside Assistance
How to Create a Histogram

1. Collect at least 50 points of continuous data.
2. Enter the date into a single column in a spreadsheet such as Excel.
3. Use your graphical package of choice to create a Histogram.

4. Add the customer specification to the Histogram to display expected vs. actual.
5. See template links below to use SigmaXL or Minitab to create a Histogram.

⚠ Potholes and Detours Around Them

Potholes	Detours
Only capturing values (mean and median) rather than creating a graph	Be sure to gather the data and create a graph. Don't rely on just the mean/average value. Get a graphical display of the data to truly understand the variation.
Poor labeling of X and Y axes	Be sure to label the X and Y axes for readability so that others understand what they're looking at.
Neglecting to mention the data and time frame being plotted	Remember to indicate what's being plotted along with when it was collected so that others know what they're looking at.

Sightseeing and Additional References

Templates:
- How to Create a Histogram in SigmaXL
- How to Create a Histogram in Minitab

Webinars:
- How to Successfully Collect Process Data for Your Lean Six Sigma Project
- 5 Ways to Create Charts & Graphs to Highlight Your Work

Single Modules:
- Histogram Training

FROM THE TRAVEL KIT:
Run Chart

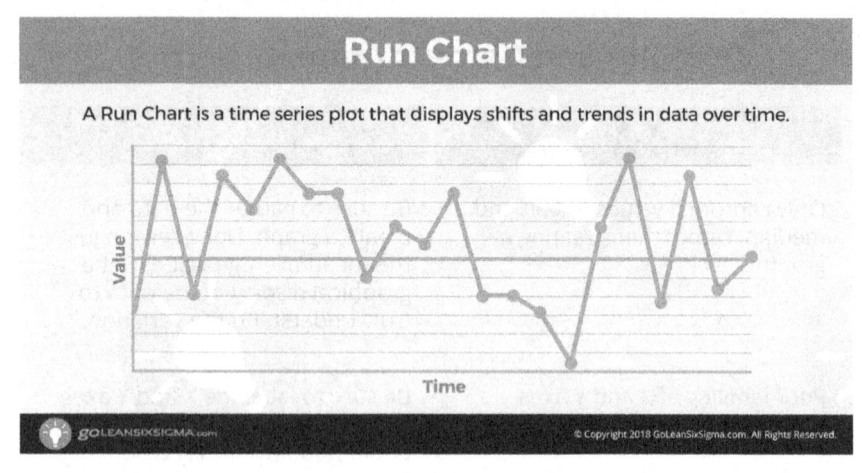

Run Chart

A Run Chart is a time series plot that displays shifts and trends in data over time.

What is a Run Chart?

A Run Chart is a time series plot that displays data in sequence over time. This kind of chart can display continuous or discrete data and generally appears with a median or average line. It's a great way to see if there are any trends or shifts in the process.

What Questions Will a Run Chart Answer?

- What's a good way to baseline my process data?
- What's a good way to show before and after data in an improvement project?
- How is the process performing over time?
- Are there any trends or shifts in the data?
- Is performance getting better, worse or staying the same?
- How much does the process vary from day to day?

Example of a Run Chart

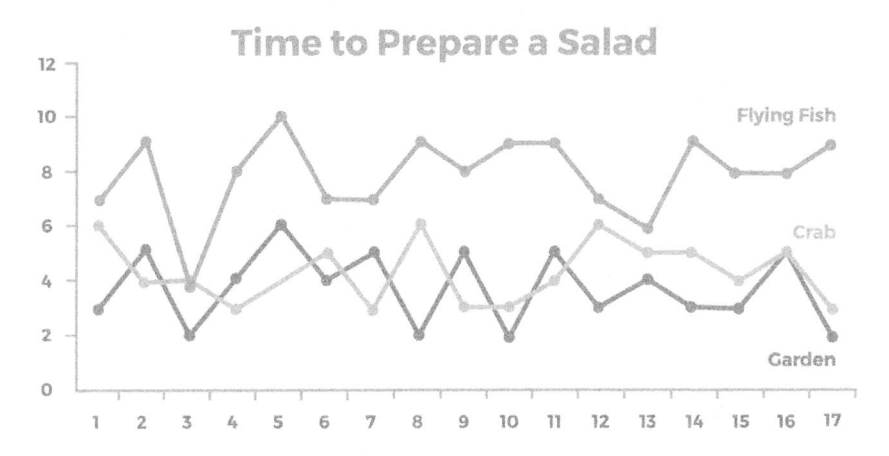

Time to Prepare a Salad

[Run chart showing three lines labeled Flying Fish, Crab, and Garden, with observations 1 through 17 on the x-axis and values 0 to 12 on the y-axis.]

When the team plotted the salad prep times, it showed Flying Fish Waldorf Salads took longer than the other salads. But nothing took over 10 minutes so it didn't seem to be a real cause of long lunch order Lead Times. But they forgot to include the prep times for the Conch Salad, so time for another chart.

Roadside Assistance
How to Create a Run Chart

1. Place your data in a column in a spreadsheet such as Excel.
2. Make sure the data is in "time order" such that the earliest observation is in the first row and the latest observation is in the last row.
3. Include the date or time of each observation in a separate column if available.
4. Use your graphical package of choice to create a Run Chart.
5. See template links below to use SigmaXL or Minitab to create a Run Chart.

Potholes and Detours Around Them

Potholes	Detours
Creating a Run Chart with less than the minimum requirement of 20 data points	Try collecting data on a more frequent basis such as weekly or daily instead of monthly.
Collecting data that creates almost a straight line	Try collecting more granular data. If you're collecting "days" you may need to move to "minutes," etc.
Discovering that the "After" Run Chart doesn't look that different from the "Before" Run Chart	Make sure you adjust the "Y" Axis minimums and maximums to be the same for each chart so you're comparing "apples to apples."
Missing what outliers might indicate	Look at data points that are particularly low or very high. If it's a good thing you might want to replicate it.

Sightseeing and Additional References

Templates:
- How to Create a Run Chart in SigmaXL
- How to Create a Run Chart in Minitab

Webinars:
- How to Successfully Collect Process Data for Your Lean Six Sigma Project
- 5 Ways to Create Charts & Graphs to Highlight Your Work

FROM THE TRAVEL KIT:
Box Plot

Box Plot

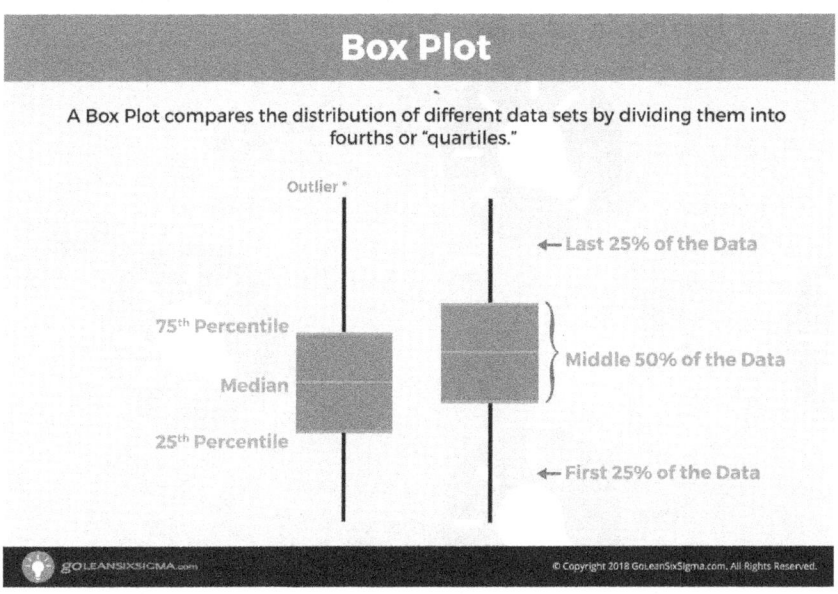

A Box Plot compares the distribution of different data sets by dividing them into fourths or "quartiles."

- Outlier *
- 75th Percentile
- Median
- 25th Percentile
- Last 25% of the Data
- Middle 50% of the Data
- First 25% of the Data

What is a Box Plot?

A Box Plot, or Box and Whisker Plot, is a graphical view of a data set that is divided into fourths or "quartiles." It shows the center and spread of a data. It shows if the data is centered or not and it includes asterisks to show any data that is outside of the norm. It is most useful when comparing two or more "strata" or data sets such as the cycle time for two different departments.

What Questions Will a Box Plot Answer?

- What's the distribution and spread of my data?
- Where is the median or center of my data set?
- What is the range of the lowest 25% of my data?
- What is the range of the top 25% of my data?

- How do the different strata or data categories compare to each other?

Example of a Box Plot

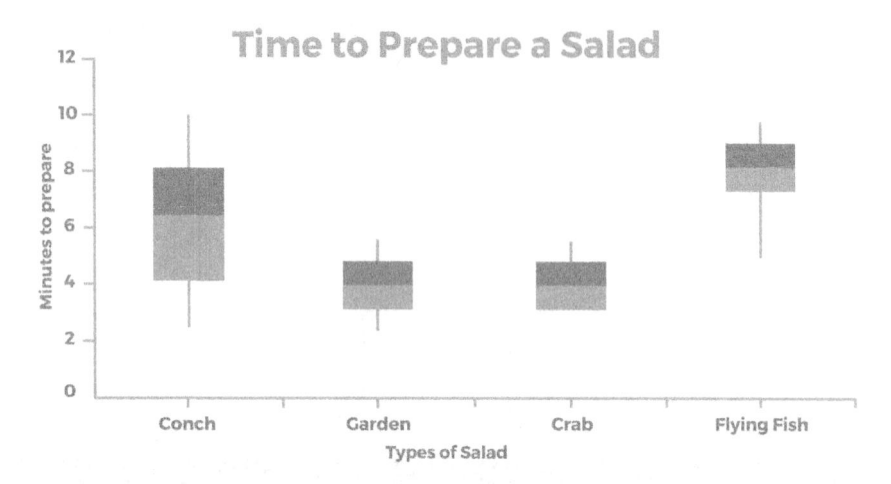

Time to Prepare a Salad

(Box plot showing Minutes to prepare (y-axis, 0 to 12) vs Types of Salad (x-axis): Conch, Garden, Crab, Flying Fish)

Once they added the Conch Salad data, the team appreciated seeing the salad preparation times side-by-side. The Box Plot made it easier to compare all of them. None of the orders went too far beyond the 10-minute mark, but the Conch Salad stood out. It had the most variation of any of the salads. They made a note to find out some tricks from the fastest prep cooks.

Roadside Assistance
How to Create a Box Plot

1. Determine which data you'd like to stratify and compare to each other.
2. Collect data for each stratification (e.g., processing time for two different employees).
3. Enter the data for each stratification into separate columns in a spreadsheet such as Excel.
4. Use your graphical package of choice to create the Box Plots

5. See links below to use SigmaXL or Minitab to create a Box Plot.

⚠ Potholes and Detours Around Them

Potholes	Detours
Creating "boxes" that are just lines with no box shape	This is caused by a data set with very similar values or only one data point for the category. Either add more data or collect more granular data (e.g., minutes instead of hours).
Creating so many boxes that they're too tiny to see	You might be trying to view too many strata. Try combining some "like" strata into single categories or pick the key strata to focus on and limit the data set.
Failing to understand the outliers	Remember to look at the data points at the extremes in order to learn why the process produces results outside the norm.

🔭 Sightseeing and Additional References

Templates:
- How to Create a Histogram in SigmaXL
- How to Create a Histogram in Minitab

Webinars:
- How to Successfully Collect Process Data for Your Lean Six Sigma Project
- 5 Ways to Create Charts & Graphs to Highlight Your Work

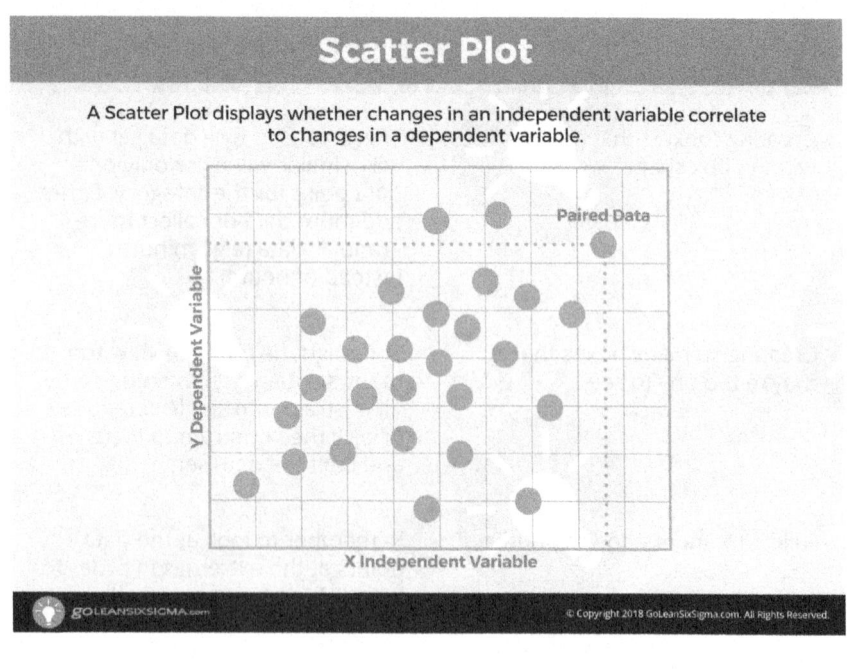

FROM THE TRAVEL KIT:
Scatter Plot

Scatter Plot

A Scatter Plot displays whether changes in an independent variable correlate to changes in a dependent variable.

What is a Scatter Plot?

A Scatter Plot is a chart that shows if there is a relationship between two variables. The resulting plot reveals whether or not changes in an independent variable "X" correlate to changes in a dependent variable "Y." It's a great way to check for root causes if you've got paired data.

What Questions Will a Scatter Plot Answer?

- Do changes in X correspond to changes in Y?
- Is there a linear correlation between two variables?
- What is the direction (positive or negative) of the correlation?
- What is the strength (weak or strong) of the correlation?

- Is this a potential "X" or root cause of the process problem?

Example of a Scatter Plot

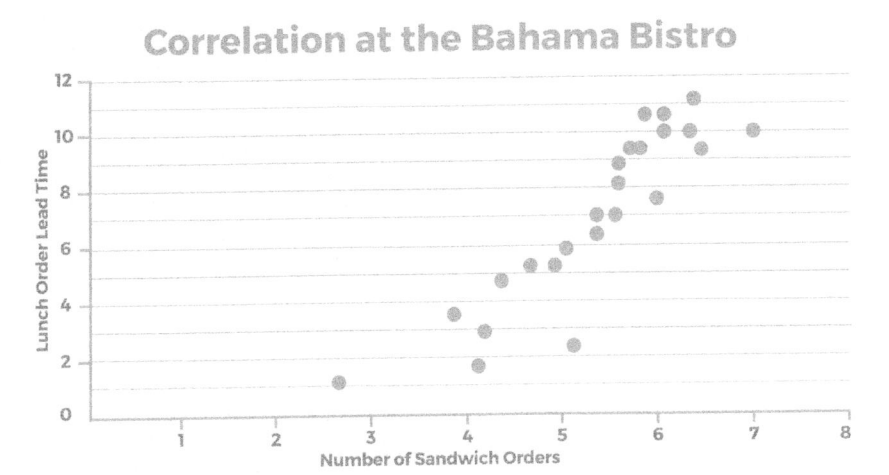

Correlation at the Bahama Bistro

Scatter plot with Y-axis "Lunch Order Lead Time" (0 to 12) and X-axis "Number of Sandwich Orders" (1 to 8), showing a positive correlation between the two variables.

The team had some paired data for the number of sandwich orders and the Lunch order Lead time. Based on the Scatter Plot, they suspected that sandwich prep time might be an issue since as sandwich orders increased so did Lunch Order Lead Time. Worthy of more investigation!

Roadside Assistance
How to Create a Scatter Plot

1. Collect X and Y "paired" data in two columns (e.g., collect the daily number of sandwich orders and pair them with the lunch order lead times for each day).
2. Enter the data into separate columns in a spreadsheet such as Excel.
3. Use the graphic package of choice to create the Scatter Plot.
4. See links below to use SigmaXL or Minitab to create a Scatter Plot.

Potholes and Detours Around Them

Potholes	Detours
Assuming that correlation means causation	Remember IQs increase with shoe size, but bigger feet are not the cause of greater intelligence!
Using discrete data instead of continuous data	Discrete data can work if there are enough distinct categories (1-10) as an option. However, this graph works best with two continuous variables.
Not using paired data	Scatter Plots require two columns of data where one data point in the first data set is related to the corresponding data point in the 2nd data set. In the example above, the number of sandwich orders for the day was paired with the average lunch order lead time for that same day.
Not using enough data resulting in a "skimpy" Scatter Plot	A general guideline is to plot a minimum of 30 paired data points.

Sightseeing and Additional References

Templates:
- How to Create a Histogram in SigmaXL
- How to Create a Histogram in Minitab

Webinars:
- How to Successfully Collect Process Data for Your Lean Six Sigma Project
- 5 Ways to Create Charts & Graphs to Highlight Your Work

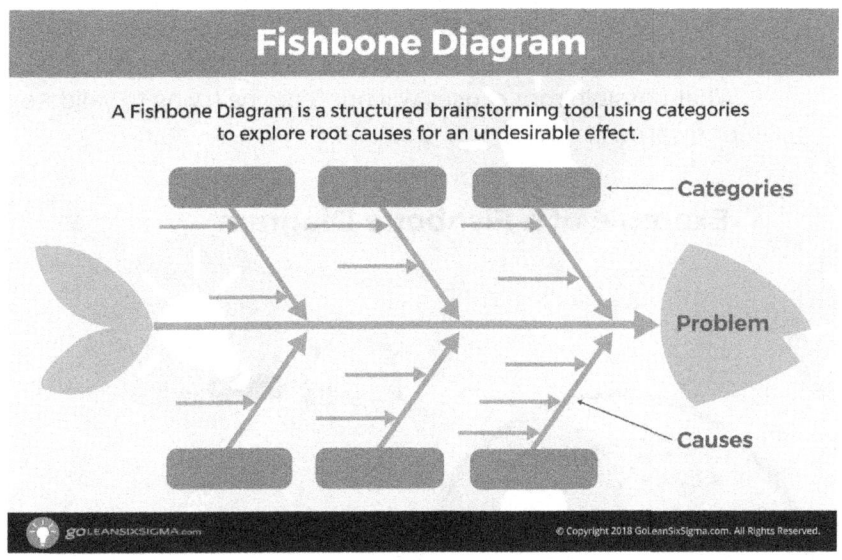

FROM THE TRAVEL KIT:
Fishbone Diagram

Fishbone Diagram

A Fishbone Diagram is a structured brainstorming tool using categories to explore root causes for an undesirable effect.

What is a Fishbone Diagram?

A Fishbone Diagram is a structured brainstorming tool designed to assist improvement teams in coming up with potential root causes for an undesirable effect. Its name derives from its resemblance to the bones of a fish. It is also known as a Cause and Effect Diagram or an Ishikawa Diagram after its creator.

Causes are often grouped into major categories, which are classically defined as the 6 Ms (or the 6 Ps): Man/Mind Power (People), Method (Process), Machines (Program), Materials (Product), Measurements (Policy) and Milieu/Mother Nature (Place).

What Questions Will a Fishbone Diagram Answer?

- What are the main categories of root causes to the problem?
- What are some of the possible root causes to the problem?
- What possible root causes will our team be trying to validate or disprove?

Example of a Fishbone Diagram

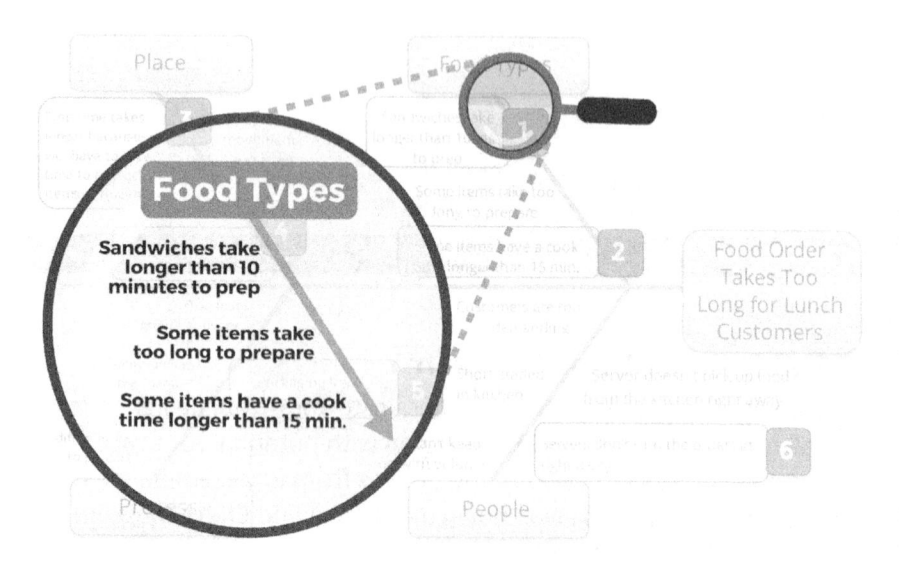

[Download Example] The whole team gathered in the back office and put paper and sticky notes on the wall. Of all the ideas they brainstormed together, they decided six of those potential root causes were worth further investigation. Sandwiches in particular seemed to deserve some extra scrutiny.

Roadside Assistance
How to Create a Fishbone Diagram

1. Download the Fishbone Diagram template.

2. Label the fish head with the problem statement, or the Project Y you are trying to improve.
3. Remember, the fish head stinks! It should be an undesirable effect or problem.
4. Two popular approaches:
    a. Brainstorm
        i. Use stickies to brainstorm possible causes
        ii. Affinitize the stickies into groups.
        iii. Use these groups as the fishbone category labels.
    b. Pre-label
        i. Apply Transactional Labels: People, Procedure, Policy, Place, Program, Product.
        ii. Apply Manufacturing Labels: Machine, Manpower, Mother Nature, Materials, Methods.
5. Once the Fishbone Diagram is populated have the team pick which primary root cause hypothesis to verify with data or process observation.
6. Circle these main root causes on your Fishbone to display the focus (shown above with numbered red circles).

Potholes and Detours Around Them

Potholes	Detours
Not putting the problem at the fish head	The fish head always stinks! The effect listed is typically your problem statement.
Not including people who truly know the process	Make sure the brainstorming team includes process experts with thoughts on cause & effect relationships.
Solutions masquerading as root causes on the Fishbone (e.g., "Lack of Training")	Be sure to brainstorm root causes vs. solutions by watching out for the phrase "Lack of..." and other indications of solutions.

Getting side-tracked with causes beyond your control	Instead of dwelling on things like weather, the economy or customers changing their minds, focus on things that are potentially actionable.
Trying to implement solutions for every potential root cause	Collect data to confirm if the hypothesis is true before focusing on solutions.

Sightseeing and Additional References

Template:
- Fishbone Diagram (aka Cause & Effect Diagram)

Blogs:
- What If IBM Used the Fishbone and 5 Whys to Fix Their Crashing Tape Drives?
- How a Cause & Effect Diagram Helped Reduce Defects by 19%
- How to Increase the Effectiveness of Your Next Cause & Effect Diagram
- Grand-Daddy of Quality: Kaoru Ishikawa

Webinar:
- How to Use a Fishbone Diagram

Single Module:
- 5 Whys & Fishbone Diagram Training

FROM THE TRAVEL KIT:
5 Whys

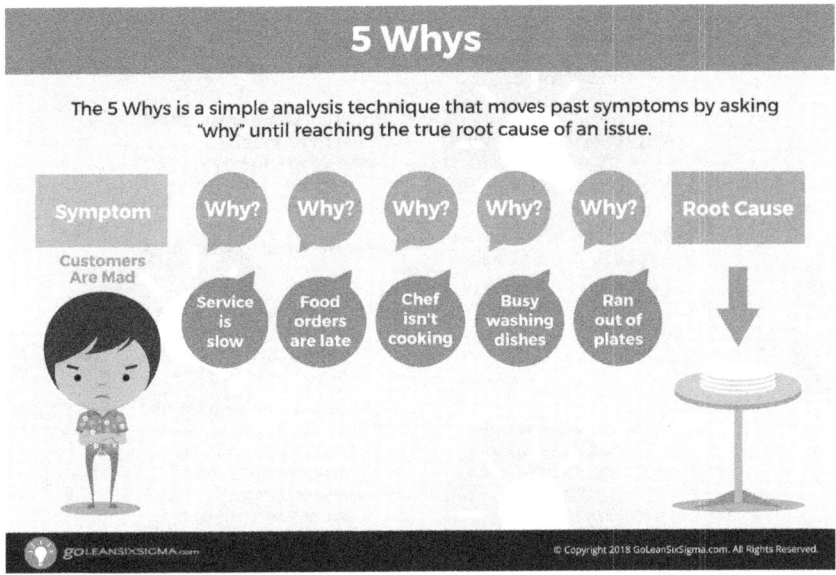

5 Whys

The 5 Whys is a simple analysis technique that moves past symptoms by asking "why" until reaching the true root cause of an issue.

Symptom: Customers Are Mad → Why? Service is slow → Why? Food orders are late → Why? Chef isn't cooking → Why? Busy washing dishes → Why? Ran out of plates → Root Cause

What are the 5 Whys?

5 Whys is a simple but effective method of analyzing and solving problems by asking "why" as many times as needed to move past symptoms and determine the true root cause of an issue. This approach is often used in tandem with the Cause-and-Effect or Fishbone Diagram.

What Questions Will the 5 Whys Answer?

- Why is this problem happening?
- What is the true root cause of this issue?
- What's a good method to dig deeper with a Fishbone (Cause & Effect) Diagram?

Example of the 5 Whys

Shift Manager's Questions	Chef's Answer
Why do the food orders take so long to deliver to the customer?	Because some of the prep takes too long.
Why does the prep take too long?	Because sometimes chefs have to re-stock supplies and wash dishes in the middle of the rush.
Why does the chef have to re-stock and wash dishes?	Because we are out of both.
Why are we out of both?	Because we don't have enough ingredients prepped and we don't have enough dishes.
Why do we not have enough prepped ingredients or enough dishes?	Because we use a lot of dishes to prep the salads, and we don't have anyone preparing back-up ingredients in case we run out.

[Download Example] The Bahama Bistro Shift Manager decided to try the 5 Whys with the Chef. They started with the main issue of food orders taking too long. By working together, they uncovered some potential disconnects between the amount of dishes prepared and the normal order volume. They decided to collect some data to get a better idea of the problem.

Roadside Assistance
How to Create the 5 Whys

1. Define a process problem.
2. Ask, "Why is this problem happening?"
3. Consider the "because" answer.
4. Ask, "Why is this happening?" again.
5. Repeat this until you reach a point where asking "why" is no longer productive.

Potholes and Detours Around Them

Potholes	Detours
Phrasing root causes as solutions such as, "lack of training, lack of automation or lack of staff" instead of actual problems	When hearing "Lack of" or similar phrases, ask what "training, automation or more staff" would solve. The real issues are more likely "knowledge level, cycle time or workload" in the case of these three common examples.
Believing that since the tool is called "5 Whys" you have to stick to that number regardless of whether the answers make sense	Consider the number "5" as an encouragement to keep digging past symptoms as opposed to an exact number of "whys" to ask.
Verifying root case at too high a level	Use the 5 Whys to get to a specific, actionable cause.
Going off course and ending up with root causes such as "there's no budget"	That indicates a solution has been inserted into the 5 Why chain (see above) which would require capital investment.

Sightseeing and Additional References

Template:
- 5 Whys

Blogs:
- What If IBM Used the Fishbone and 5 Whys to Fix Their Crashing Tape Drives?
- Grand-Daddy of Quality: Sakichi Toyoda

Webinars:
- Challenge the Process by Asking "Why?"
- How to Use a Fishbone Diagram

Single Module:
- 5 Whys & Fishbone Diagram Training

FROM THE TRAVEL KIT:
Root Cause Hypothesis Statement

Root Cause Hypothesis Statement

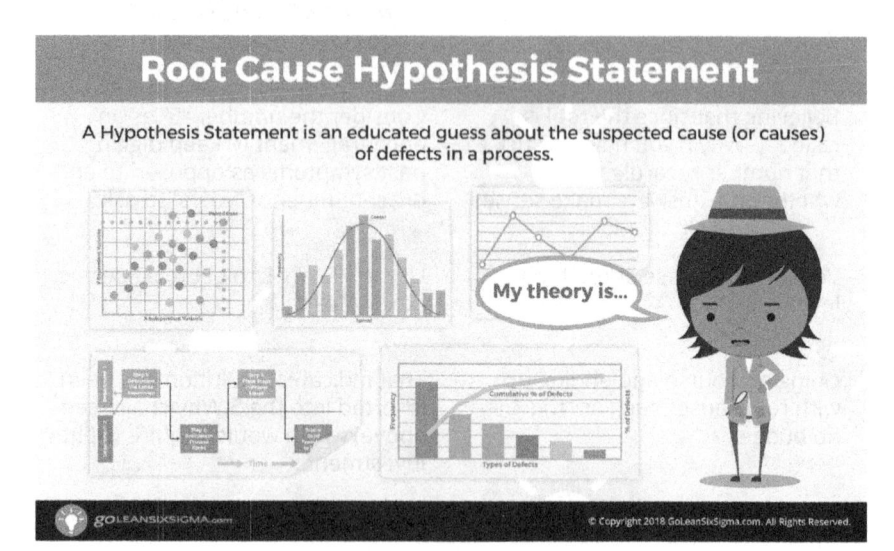

A Hypothesis Statement is an educated guess about the suspected cause (or causes) of defects in a process.

My theory is...

What is a Root Cause Hypothesis Statement?

Root Cause Hypothesis is an educated guess as to the cause of a problem in a process. Root Cause Hypothesis Statements are part of the Analyze Phase in DMAIC. In order to form Hypotheses regarding the causes of process issues, one must conduct Root Cause Analysis, which involves questioning and investigating to move past symptoms to the true root of the problem.

What Questions Will a Root Cause Hypothesis Statement Answer?

- What are some of the reasons this problem is happening?
- How can we phrase our root cause theories in the form of hypothesis statements?
- Which root cause hypotheses are true?
- Which root cause hypotheses are false?
- What kind of verification do we have regarding whether the hypotheses are true or false?

Example of Root Cause Hypotheses

Hypothesis	Possible Root Cause(s)	Root Cause Hypothesis
1	Preparation Time	Sandwiches take too long to prep, too much time spent on gathering items
2	Cook Time	Some of the lunch items have a cook time longer than 20 minutes
3	Preparation Time	Many times, needed items are not stocked enough to carry through the lunch hour. Kitchen staff waste time gathering items intead of preparing meals.
4	Preparation Time	Prep area not very well organized
5	Packaging Time	Packaging items for pick-up is cumbersome and time-consuming
6	Server	The server doesn't turn the order in to the kitchen right away

[Download Example] The team realized that preparation time was becoming a common theme as a root cause although they had different theories. Each theory would require different data for verification so spelling out the different hypotheses was critical.

Roadside Assistance
How to Create a Root Cause Hypothesis Statement

1. Download the Root Cause Hypothesis template.
2. Work with your team to filter and select the root causes listed on the Fishbone Diagram that are worth proving or disproving.
3. Use the Root Cause Hypothesis template to capture the shortened list of potential root causes.
4. Under "Possible Root Cause" enter the "X" that is the factor involved in causing the issue for each hypothesis.
    a. The possible root cause (the "X") is typically a noun.
    b. Use just one or two words to describe the "X."
5. Under "Root Cause Hypothesis Statements" enter each theory of root cause.
    a. The root cause hypothesis is typically a sentence.
    b. You could have more than one hypothesis per potential root cause since it's not necessarily a one-to-one ratio.
    c. Example: The hypothesis statement for Preparation Time is "Sandwiches take too long to prep," but another possible hypothesis statement for Preparation Time could be, "Some items take much longer to prepare than others."
    d. In cases with two theories for a single "X," simply list the root cause on another line with the 2nd hypothesis statement.
6. Under "Verification" list the the graph, data or method used to verify each hypothesis.
7. Under "Result" enter "True" or "False" based on whether you proved or disproved the hypothesis.

Potholes and Detours Around Them

Potholes	Detours
Not having any possible root causes to research and prove	Reassess your Project Charter. Do you have a solution already identified? If so, you may need to abandon DMAIC and complete this as a Quick Win.
Having difficulty figuring out how to prove/disprove the root causes	There are two ways to prove/disprove hypothesis: data analysis and process analysis. Start with one of these choices and go from there.
Listing True or False but having no evidence or proof	Stick with it. This can be the most difficult step, but it is the most important step in DMAIC. Proving root cause will provide you with confirmation and a clearer path to solving the problem for good.

Sightseeing and Additional References

Template:
- Root Cause Hypothesis

Analyze Phase: Summary

The Analyze Phase separates "change for change's sake" from worthwhile improvement efforts. This phase generally results in unplanned detours. You might have to look under the hood of the car and get a little grease on your hands!

If you've spent some time digging into the process and the data, you've probably made some great discoveries. Breakthrough improvements require that you focus your efforts here. You need to strike a delicate balance between analysis paralysis and "gut instinct" changes. If you think you're ready, the next phase is like a trip to the amusement park. Got your tickets?

Analyze Phase Challenges

- Spending the time needed to explore root causes
- Getting caught up in analysis paralysis
- Jumping to solutions without confirming root cause hypothesis
- Collecting the right data to confirm or validate hypothesis

Analyze Phase Best Practices

- Fill out the Fishbone Diagram with a group — it's another opportunity for engagement.
- Use all opportunities to get to root cause — data, observations, interviews, process maps, etc.
- Document the verification of root cause even if it's just an observation.
- Update stakeholders on all findings — communicate often.

Journey Journaling

Do you like the word "Hypothesis?" Did the Fishbone Diagram make you think of fishcakes? Time to ask yourself a few questions:
- Are you satisfied that you know enough about the root causes to start solving the problem?
- Are you sure you're not jumping to solution?
- Want to jot down some notes about your progress?
- What lessons did you learn?
- What would you do differently next time?

Analyze Phase Journey

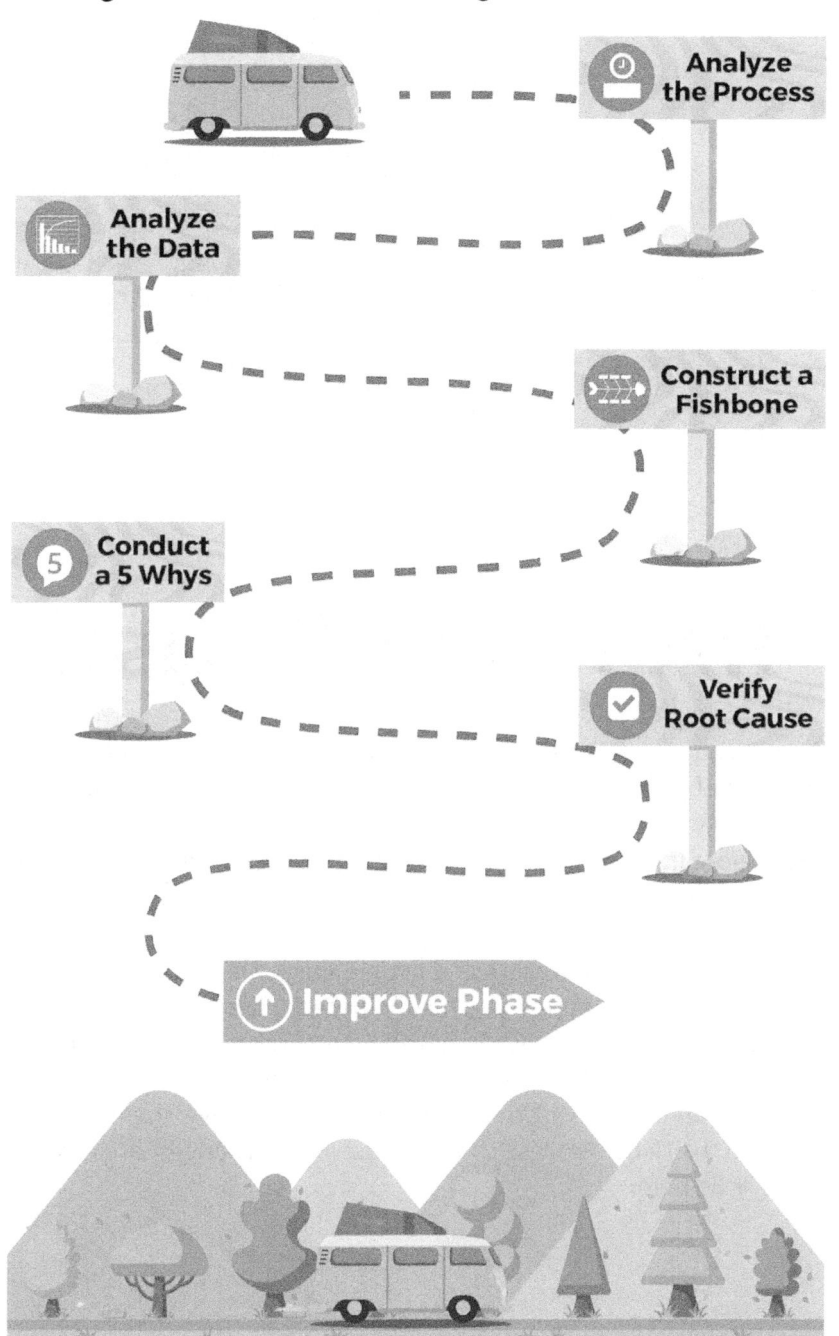

- Analyze the Process
- Analyze the Data
- Construct a Fishbone
- Conduct a 5 Whys
- Verify Root Cause
- ↑ Improve Phase

Improve Phase

Once through the Analyze Phase, the trip picks up speed. This stretch of the road is fun! You figured out the source of the problem and now you get to fix it. Countermeasures might involve simplifying a form, reorganizing a workspace, skipping a review — the options are endless! The trick is to test each solution and work out the kinks.

Work with your stakeholders and get feedback. Depending on the root cause, you might find you need different passengers. You probably want to keep travelling with your current crew, but your work won't be as effective if you don't include the right people. Don't keep the fun to yourself! The more people you involve, the more engaged they'll be. Process changes, just like oil changes, are easier with a little help.

STEPS IN THE IMPROVE PHASE

Craft Solutions

Combine discoveries, brainstorming and the Solution Parking Lot to develop a robust list of potential countermeasures to choose from.

Filter Solutions

Work to assess the best of the high-impact/low-effort solutions to devote time and energy to.

Determine Solution Approaches

Figure out how to test, tweak and rollout each change to minimize disruption and guarantee improved process capability.

Conduct Risk Management

Work with the team to assess and plan for the unintended consequences of changing the process.

IMPROVE PHASE TRAVEL KIT — WHAT'S INSIDE:

5S
5S is a five-step organizing technique to create and maintain an intuitive workspace.

Work Cell Design
Work Cell Design organizes a workspace by process flow rather than function to minimize transportation, motion and waiting.

Kanban
A Kanban is a visual signal that triggers an action, typically to make a unit, move a unit or order a unit.

Solution Selection Matrix
The Solution Selection Matrix ranks each proposed countermeasure for its ability to solve a problem and the level of effort required.

FMEA
Failure Modes & Effects Analysis (FMEA) is a risk management tool that identifies and quantifies the influence of potential failures in a process in order to prevent them or create contingency plans.

FROM THE TRAVEL KIT:
5S

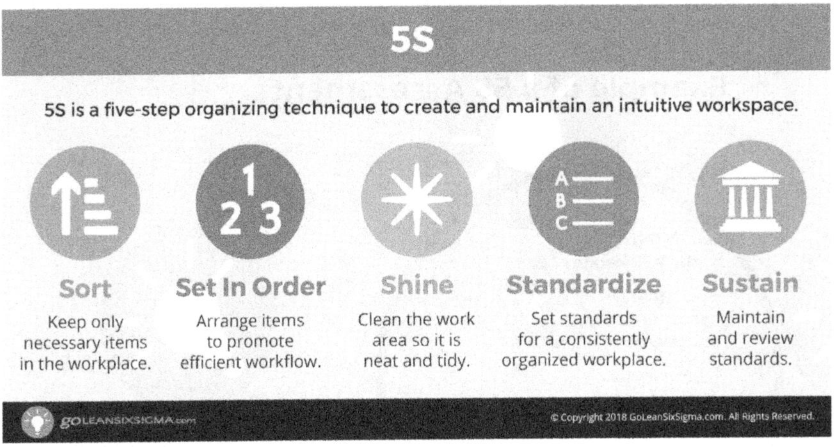

5S

5S is a five-step organizing technique to create and maintain an intuitive workspace.

Sort	Set In Order	Shine	Standardize	Sustain
Keep only necessary items in the workplace.	Arrange items to promote efficient workflow.	Clean the work area so it is neat and tidy.	Set standards for a consistently organized workplace.	Maintain and review standards.

goLEANSIXSIGMA.com © Copyright 2018 GoLeanSixSigma.com. All Rights Reserved.

What is a 5S?

5S is a five-step organizing technique that guides participants on how to create and maintain an intuitive workspace. The process begins with removing anything the group doesn't really need, putting supplies and materials where they're easiest to access and then cleaning up the workspace.

The last 2 steps are devoted to setting up the ongoing standards for the space and then implementing audits to maintain the organization. The last 2 are the tough part but critical to keep a 5S from turning into a "once-in-a-blue-moon" 3S!

What Questions Will a 5S Answer?

- How can I create an intuitive workspace?
- What files, materials or supplies can I remove?
- What's the right amount of supplies or files to keep on hand?
- Where's the best place to stow materials or files?
- How can we keep this workspace in order?

- What visuals will help people navigate this workspace?
- What's a good way to show people the process flow?
- Who should be in charge of maintaining this workspace?
- How often should we audit this workspace?

Example of a 5S Assessment

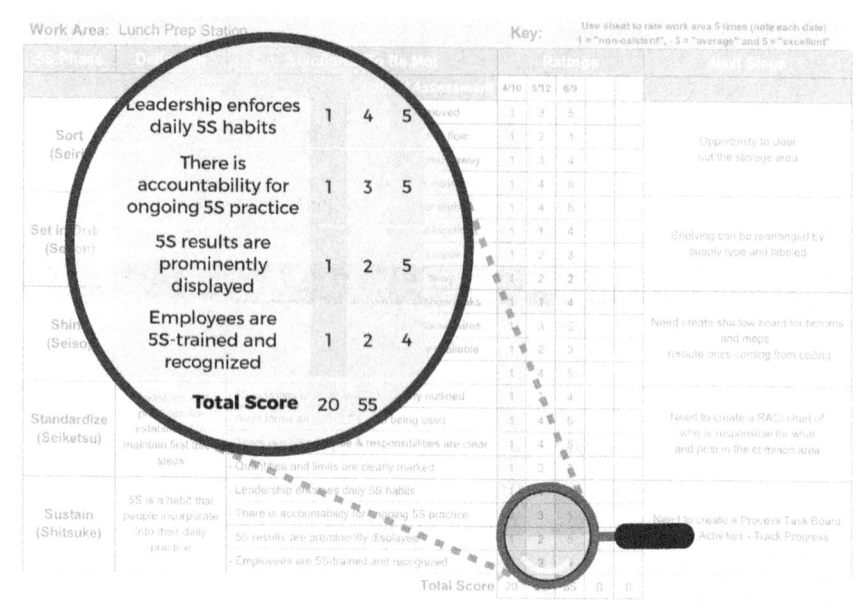

[Image of a 5S Assessment worksheet with a magnified callout showing:]

- Leadership enforces daily 5S habits — 1, 4, 5
- There is accountability for ongoing 5S practice — 1, 3, 5
- 5S results are prominently displayed — 1, 2, 5
- Employees are 5S-trained and recognized — 1, 2, 4
- Total Score: 20, 55

[Download Example] Since the team had confirmed theories about preparation being a root cause, it made sense to conduct a 5S of the Lunch Prep Station. They key to sustaining the newly organized workspace was to audit and score it each month. They were steadily getting better because everyone worked to keep up the 5S Score!

Roadside Assistance
How to Conduct a 5S

1. Download the Transactional or Manufacturing 5S Assessment template.
2. Choose a workspace — physical or digital — to organize
3. Conduct an audit of the workspace to establish a baseline

a. Use either the Transactional or Manufacturing 5S Check Sheets (see below).
4. Take pictures or screenshots to establish a visual baseline.
5. Sort:
    a. Remove unneeded items from the workspace.
    b. Keep only what's essential in the quantities needed.
6. Set In Order:
    a. Arrange items so they are easily accessible.
    b. Follow the saying, "A place for everything, and everything in its place."
    c. Use labels to make it obvious where things go and where to find them.
7. Shine:
    a. Clean the work area so it is neat and tidy.
    b. In the case of a digital space, this would refer to IT maintenance.
8. Standardize:
    a. Set standards for a consistently organized workplace.
    b. Make standards easy to understand.
    c. Set a schedule and accountability for regular audits.
9. Sustain:
    a. Maintain and review standards.
    b. Address root causes and avoid reversion to "old ways."
10. Post "Before" and "After" pictures to maintain awareness of the improvement achieved and the current standard.

Potholes and Detours Around Them

Potholes	Detours
Conducting a "3S" instead of a 5S and without regular maintenance, it slips into disorganization	Leadership has to make accountability clear for sustaining the standards with regular audits.
"Customizing" a previously 5Sed workspace without coordinating with others and causing confusion	Make sure labels are clear and "Before" and "After" pictures are visible. Check to ensure everyone

	is adhering to standards during the regular audit.
Assuming improvements are not allowed once a workspace has gone through a 5S	5S is a continuous improvement technique which means there's always room for refinement. Be sure to incorporate updates to the standards if they work for everyone using the workspace.
Conducting a 5S when other actions are more appropriate	5S can be an "activity trap" that diverts you from what is really needed. If you are delivering late to the customer, housekeeping may not be the top priority.

Sightseeing and Additional References

Templates:
- 5S Manufacturing Assessment
- 5S Transactional Assessment

Blogs:
- How to Apply 5S: Elementary School Classroom
- How to Apply 5S: The Frightening Fridge at Work

Webinar:
- How to Harness the Power of 5S and Visual Management

Single Module:
- 5S Training

FROM THE TRAVEL KIT:
Work Cell Design

Work Cell Design

Work Cell Design organizes a workspace by process flow rather than function to minimize transportation, motion and waiting.

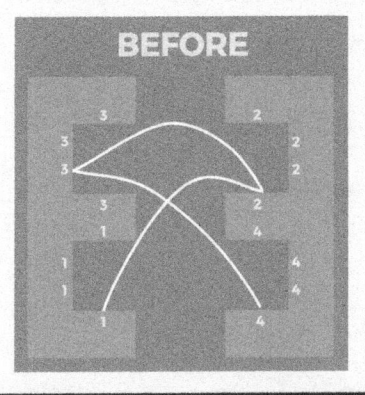

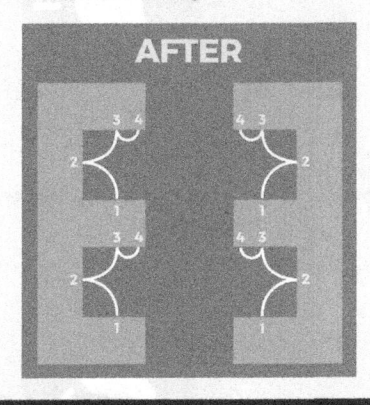

BEFORE / **AFTER**

What is Work Cell Design?

Work Cell Design is a method of organizing physical operations by process flow as opposed to function in order remove barriers between work groups and maximize value-added steps. The most classically efficient work space shape is the U-shape which minimizes the wastes of transportation, motion and waiting. Work Cells become smaller and cross-functional while work moves faster.

What Questions Will Work Cell Design Answer?

- How do we design a process that minimizes waste (motion, transportation and waiting) and maximizes process flow?
- How can we shorten the distances people have to walk?

- How can we move materials or tools closer to where the work takes place?
- How do we arrange work by the process flow as opposed to functions and departments?

📝 Example of a Work Cell

Combo Lunch Order Layout

Salad Station → Soup Station → Sandwich Station

Combo Work Cell Layout

One great opportunity for implementing the Work Cell was the different prep stations for combo lunch orders. Having to walk between the different areas took time and separated the orders. This way the team formed one happy pod and cranked out combo lunch orders together!

🅰 Roadside Assistance
How to Design a Work Cell

1. Identify the process or the product to be organized into a Work Cell.
2. Conduct a time study on the process flow and determine the number of people and equipment needed.

3. Balance the workload within the cell in order to eliminate barriers to flow and remove bottlenecks.
4. Determine the best physical arrangement of tasks, people and equipment.
5. Continue to self-improve the Work Cell for maximum efficiency and effectiveness.

Potholes and Detours Around Them

Potholes	Detours
Creating a Work Cell for only one function or section	Ideally, a Work Cell combines multiple functions to reduce handoffs and waiting.
Creating an uneven workload within the Work Cell	Be sure the workload is balanced to minimize frustration and bottlenecks in the Work Cell.
Using a "One-and-Done" approach — setting up the Work Cell and moving onto something else	Be sure to re-assess and experiment with the Work Cell. Don't forget to check and adjust as needed.
Giving up because a particular machine or piece of equipment cannot be moved	Design a cell with that machine in its current location and move other machines and workstations around it.

Sightseeing and Additional References

Template:
- Spaghetti Map

FROM THE TRAVEL KIT:
Kanban

Kanban

A Kanban is a visual signal that triggers an action, typically to make a unit, move a unit, or order a unit.

Lizzy O'Rourke
123 Kaneohe Lane
Nassau, Bahamas

000123
REF-01234

IT'S TIME TO REORDER CHECKS!

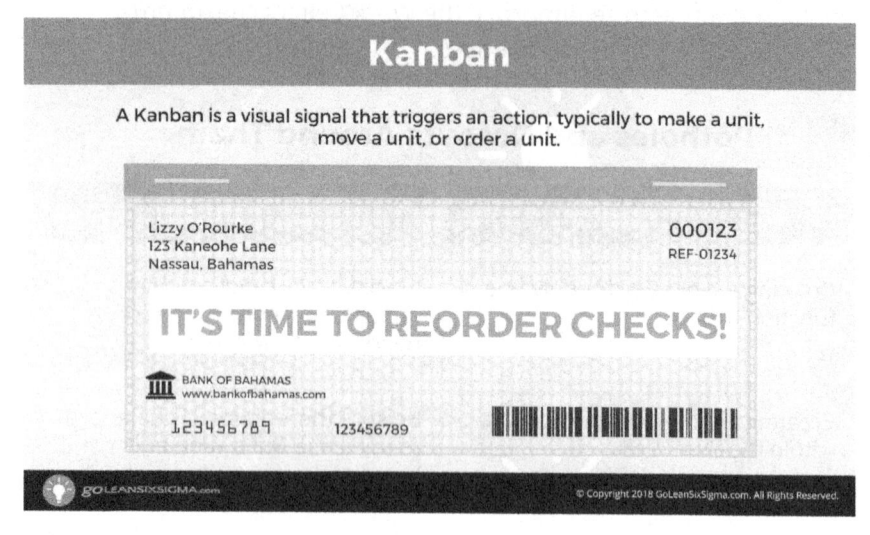

BANK OF BAHAMAS
www.bankofbahamas.com

123456789   123456789

What is a Kanban?

Kanban is a Japanese term that translates to "card" or "board" and indicates a signal for action within a process. Kanbans are part of Just-In-Time (JIT) processing where either a physical or electronic device indicates that it's time to order inventory, process a unit or move to the next step in a process.

What Questions Will a Kanban Answer?

- How many items have been purchased or moved?
- When should I order more?
- When should I move or make a unit?
- When should I place an order?

Example of a Kanban

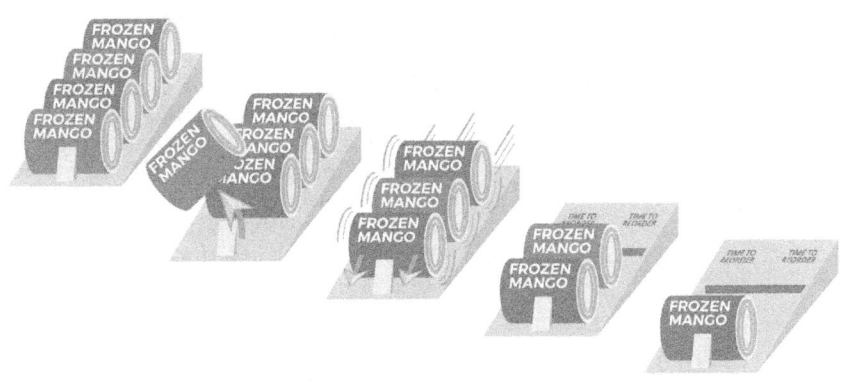

The team is familiar with the Kanban concept since they use it in the walk-in freezer. They set up the shelving so that canned goods roll into place when they take one out. The red lines tell them when to reorder so they never run out!

Roadside Assistance
How to Create a Kanban

1. Determine the process or product to design a Kanban(s).
2. Determine if a 1- or 2-bin system will be used (or other).
3. Determine bin size quantity using the formula to determine the right quantity.
4. Pilot the Kanban and adjust where needed.

Potholes and Detours Around Them

Potholes	Detours
Running out of inventory	Adjust your bin size and don't forget to include the safety stock.

| Creating too much inventory | Adjust your bin size and remember to only order safety stock at the beginning; don't replenish on every order. |
| Losing Kanban triggers | Make sure everyone involved in the process knows that when a Kanban trigger is reached, it must be conveyed immediately for replenishment. Caution people that losing the cards (or boards) could result in a stockout. |

Sightseeing and Additional References

Blog:
- How I Solved My Shoe Addiction Using Lean Six Sigma

FROM THE TRAVEL KIT:
Solution Selection Matrix

Solution Selection Matrix

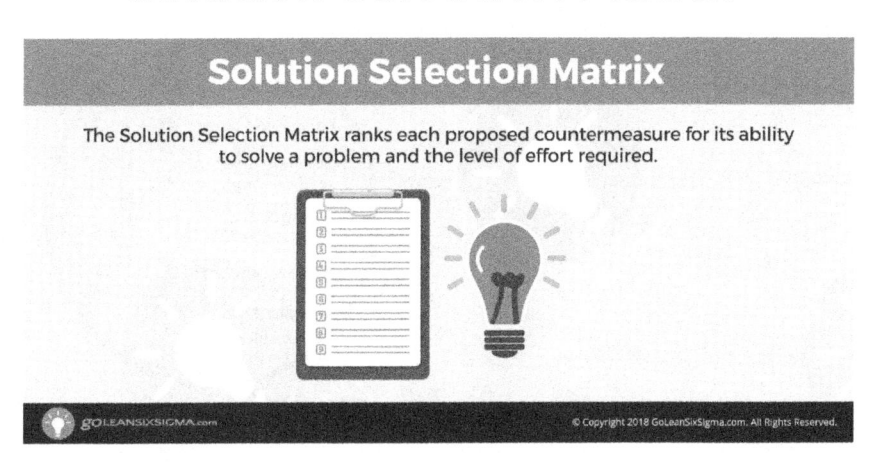

The Solution Selection Matrix ranks each proposed countermeasure for its ability to solve a problem and the level of effort required.

What is a Solution Selection Matrix?

The Solution Selection Matrix provides a method of ranking the positive impact of each proposed solution as well as the relative effort, time and cost involved for each idea. Improvement teams rate each solution based on key criteria resulting in cumulative scores and then they indicate whether or not they chose to implement each solution.

What Questions Will a Solution Selection Matrix Answer?

- How will this solution impact our ability to reach the goal?
- How much benefit will the customer experience with this solution?
- How much money will this cost to implement?
- Is there buy-in from stakeholders for this idea?
- How long would it take to implement this solution?
- What are the best solution(s)?
- Which of these solutions should I implement?

Example of a Solution Selection Matrix

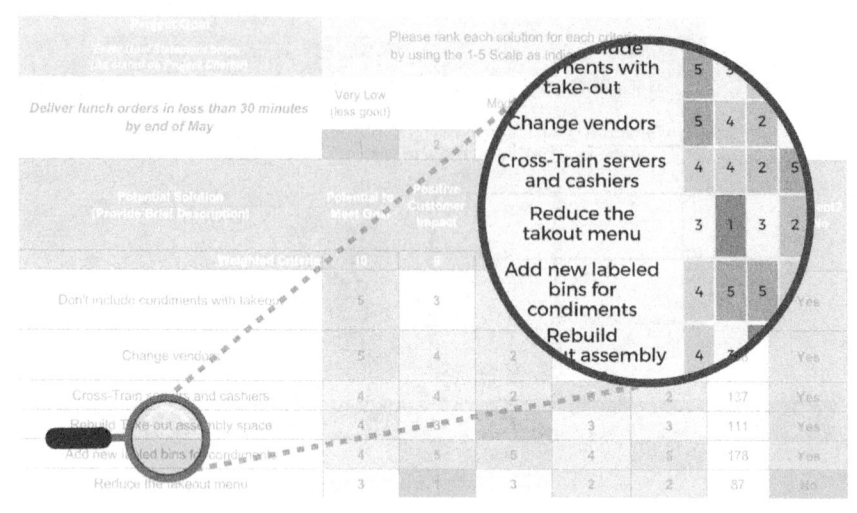

[Download Example] The team had lots of great ideas but it helped to consider the cost and impact on the customer along with each idea's ability to help meet their project goal. They opted for almost everything, but they decided against reducing the takeout menu since customers love the menu options and it wouldn't have a big impact on reducing lead time.

Roadside Assistance
How to Complete a Solution Selection Matrix

1. Download the Solution Selection Matrix template.
2. Enter the project goal in the space provided.
3. List all solution ideas in the first column.
4. Rate each solution based on the 5 criteria provided.
5. Notice the total scores for the list.
6. Determine which solutions to implement and enter either "Yes" or "No" based on those decisions.

Potholes and Detours Around Them

Potholes	Detours
Inserting a generic goal such as "streamline the process" so it's hard to rank using the specified criteria	Make sure the goal has been copied verbatim from the Project Charter so that it's specific and measurable.
Scoring a "1" for "Cost to Implement," which translates to most expensive, but the solution being scored is free	People forget that when dealing with "Cost," a high cost receives a low number. It's counter-intuitive, so double-check all the "Cost" scores.
Placing a different value on the weighted criteria than those provided	The weighted criteria are suggestions and can be customized to suit the organization.

Sightseeing and Additional References

Template:
- Solution Selection Matrix

FROM THE TRAVEL KIT:
Failure Modes & Effects Analysis (FMEA)

Failure Modes & Effects Analysis

Failure Modes & Effects Analysis (FMEA) is a risk management tool that identifies the influence of potential failures in a process in order to prevent them or create contingency plans.

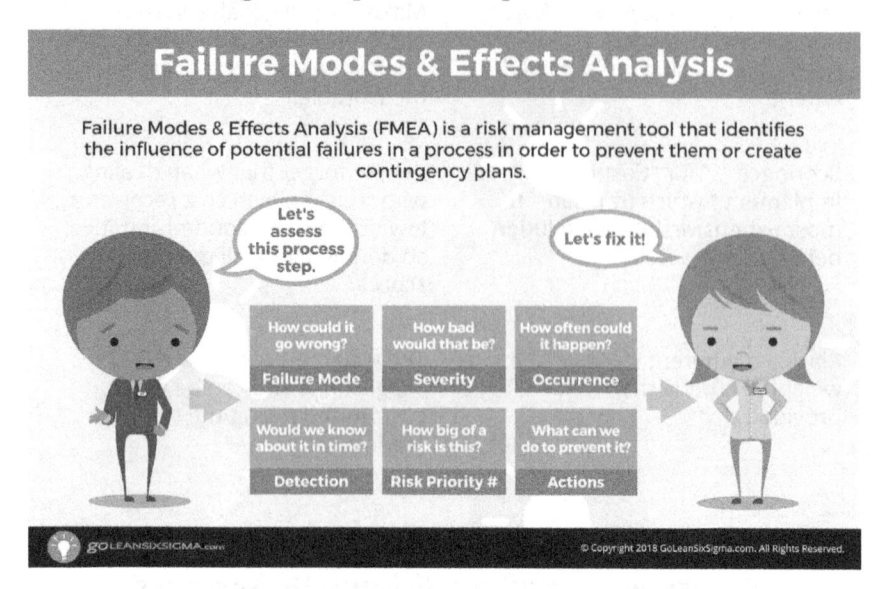

Failure Mode	Severity	Occurrence
How could it go wrong?	How bad would that be?	How often could it happen?

Detection	Risk Priority #	Actions
Would we know about it in time?	How big of a risk is this?	What can we do to prevent it?

What is an FMEA?

Failure Modes & Effects Analysis (FMEA) is a risk management tool that identifies and quantifies the influence of potential failures in a process. FMEA analyzes potential failures using three criteria:

1. Occurrence (failure cause and frequency)
2. Severity (impact of the failure)
3. Detection (likelihood of failure detection)

Once assessed, prioritized failures are addressed with mistake-proofing for preventable failures and contingency plans for unpreventable risks.

What Questions Will an FMEA Answer?

- What are the biggest risks of failure existing in this process?
- What is the risk of removing or changing a step?
- Are there any risks associated with proposed solutions?
- How can I prevent failures from happening at all?
- What are some good contingency plans for things that can't be prevented?
- How can I reduce the severity of potential failures?
- How can I reduce the frequency of potential failures?
- How can I make it easier to detect failures before they impact the customer?
- Who will implement risk mitigation and when?

Example of an FMEA

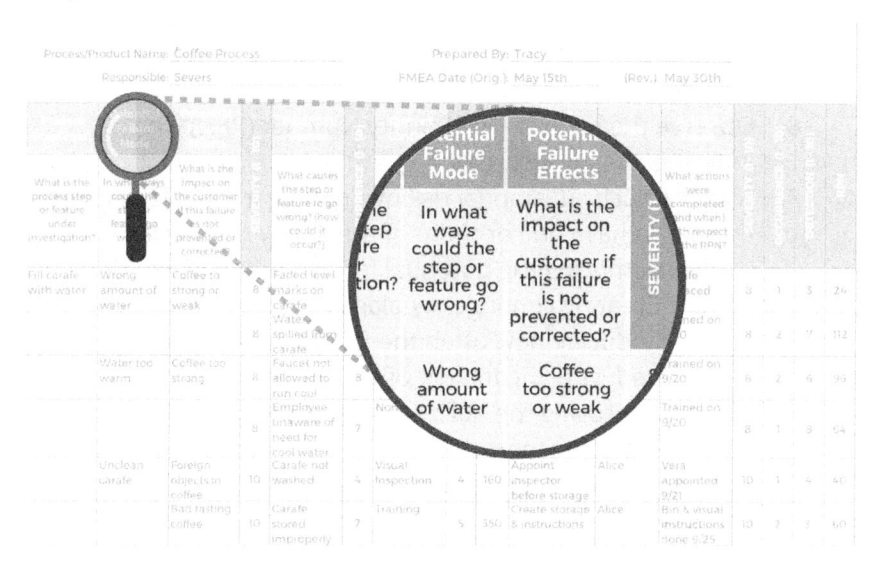

[Download Example] While the team was working on the Lunch Order Lead time, their new coffee machine got delivered. Since it had potential to cause unintended consequences, they decided to try out the FMEA on the new machine. Weak coffee disaster averted!

Roadside Assistance
How to Create an FMEA

1. Download the FMEA template.
2. View and customize each of the 3 default scales to suit the process being examined (see tabs for each).
3. Determine which step, change or feature to assess (either existing or new to the process).
4. Brainstorm different ways that step, feature or change could fail.
5. Describe the impact of each potential failure; rate the impact of each failure using the "Severity" Scale.
6. Describe what could cause each potential failure; rate how often each failure might occur based on the "Occurrence" Scale.
7. Describe how difficult it would be to detect the failure before it impacted the customer; rate the ability to detect failures on the "Detection" Scale.
8. Observe the highest Risk Priority Number (RPN) which indicates the biggest risk.
9. Address each substantial risk by devising a countermeasure that could have one or more of the following effects:
    a. Removing the potential for the failure altogether
    b. Creating contingency plans for unpreventable failures
    c. Reducing how often the failure could happen
    d. Reducing the impact of the potential failure
    e. Improving the ability to detect the failure before it impacts others
10. Set a date and assign responsibility for implementing each countermeasure.
11. Adjust the ratings for Severity, Occurrence and Detection and recalculate the new Risk Priority Number.

Potholes and Detours Around Them

Potholes	Detours
Assuming the template requires one line per step and missing potential failures and impacts	Be sure to brainstorm all potential failures and list them on separate rows. Be aware that there could be multiple effects or causes and list them separately.
Assuming the FMEA is exclusively for existing processes or, conversely, that it's only for "To Be" processes	Remember that the tool is good for mitigating risk in both existing and "to be" processes.
Completing the first half of the FMEA but neglecting to come up with action plans to reduce the risk of failure in the process	Be sure to create action plans to eliminate or plan for the biggest risks and then recalculate the Risk Priority Number to see how much the risk has been reduced.
Assuming the default Severity, Occurrence and Detection scales are required even if they don't apply to the process	The scales provided are generic and should always be customized to address the process being studied.
Executing the FMEA without assistance and missing potential risks	Whether in person or online, the FMEA becomes more useful as more process participants weigh in with their process knowledge.
Reducing the Severity after the "Actions" section without appropriate cause	Usually follow-up actions improve the Occurrence or Detection. Typically Severity is not impacted unless you fundamentally change the nature of the failure mode (e.g., failing in a less severe manner).

Sightseeing and Additional References

Template:
- Failure Modes & Effects Analysis (FMEA)

Blog:
- How to Turn Unintended Consequences Into Happy Accidents Using Lean Six Sigma

Webinar:
- How to Effectively Avoid Unintended Project Consequences Using FMEA

Single Module:
- FMEA Training

Improve Phase: Summary

We've been on the journey for a while but this is where the magic happens. This phase is so much fun people can't stay away even when they're still baselining the process! Of course, it's important to tend to the obvious Quick Wins when it makes sense. Hopefully you got to try out ideas from everyone who's come in contact with the project.

It's hard to beat the satisfaction of making a positive impact. Get out of the car, stretch your legs and take a moment to appreciate your efforts. Thank your contributors and give everyone involved some credit and appreciation (it's free).

When you're ready, there's one more stop to make. Time to ensure the new process "sticks" and that the pursuit of perfection continues with new experiments.

Improve Phase Challenges

- Involving the right people
- Increasing workload if there are multiple root causes
- Avoiding "pet" solutions that may not address any root cause
- Dealing with increased resistance when people realize their area is about to undergo change

Improve Phase Best Practices

- Invite stakeholders to brainstorm solutions - another opportunity for engagement.
- Steal shamelessly — review common solutions or find who else has solved a similar issue.
- Conduct a 5S if you have not already — physical, digital or both for easy wins.
- Make it easy for people to follow the new process — use visuals and mistake-proofing.

Journey Journaling

Wasn't that great? Want to do that phase again? That's not a bad idea! Time to ask yourself a few questions:

- Are people excited about the changes?
- Are they giving you more ideas??
- Did you see measurable improvement in the process?
- What lessons did you learn?
- What would you do differently next time?

Improve Phase Journey

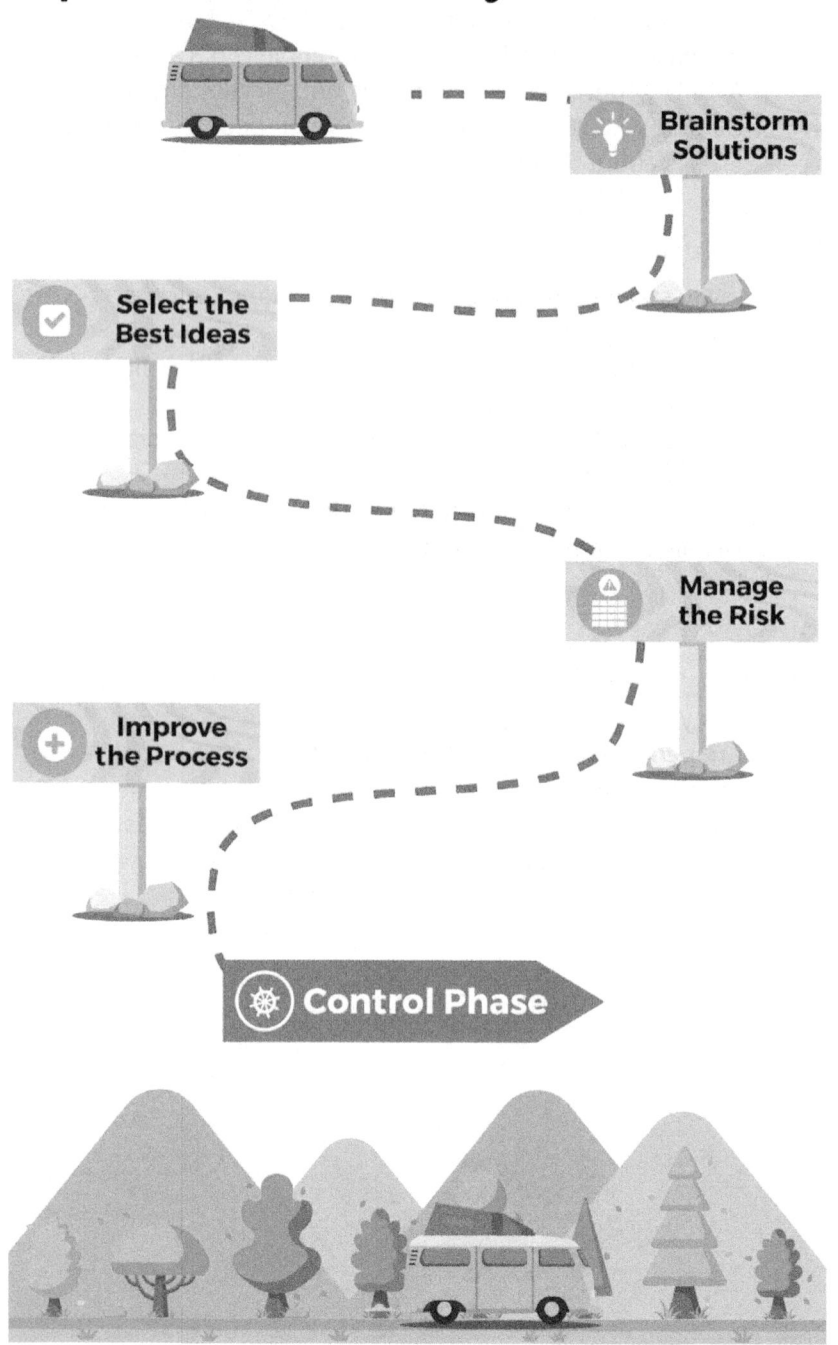

- Brainstorm Solutions
- Select the Best Ideas
- Manage the Risk
- Improve the Process
- Control Phase

Control Phase

As exciting as the Improve Phase was, the Control Phase tends to suffer by comparison. It's like cleaning your glasses, making sure you have your wallet and topping off the tank. Not exactly glamorous, but without these you might end up wandering penniless along the side of the road. Your project deserves the best!

It's not just the "Control Phase" — it's the "Continue Phase." Everyone in the car is reflecting on the project success with smiles of satisfaction but it's never the "end." Your fellow travellers are in good spirits so this is the perfect time to ensure you sustain the gains and pave the way for continuous improvement.

You're almost there!

STEPS IN THE CONTROL PHASE

Create Monitoring Plans

Work with the Process Owner to select measures and plan to keep an eye on the performance of the improved process.

Develop Response Plans

Decide what you want people to do if there's a noticeable slip in process performance and how to continue with improvements.

Document the Project

Capture the elements of the project such that others can learn from you.

Pursue Perfection

Process improvement is an ongoing, never-ending cycle, so you should always be thinking about "What's next?"

CONTROL PHASE TRAVEL KIT — WHAT'S INSIDE:

Monitoring & Response Plan
The Monitoring & Response Plan checks whether a process is performing as expected and details what to do if not.

Executive Summary
The Executive Summary uses the A3 format to summarize the business case, the goal, the root causes, the improvements, the benefits and then display the "before" and "after" status of the Project Y.

Project Storyboard
Project Storyboards are ready-to-go project overviews.

Innovation Transfer
Innovation Transfer is the effort to take all or part of a successful solution and apply it elsewhere in the organization.

The Next Project
Continuous Improvement is…continuous!

FROM THE TRAVEL KIT:

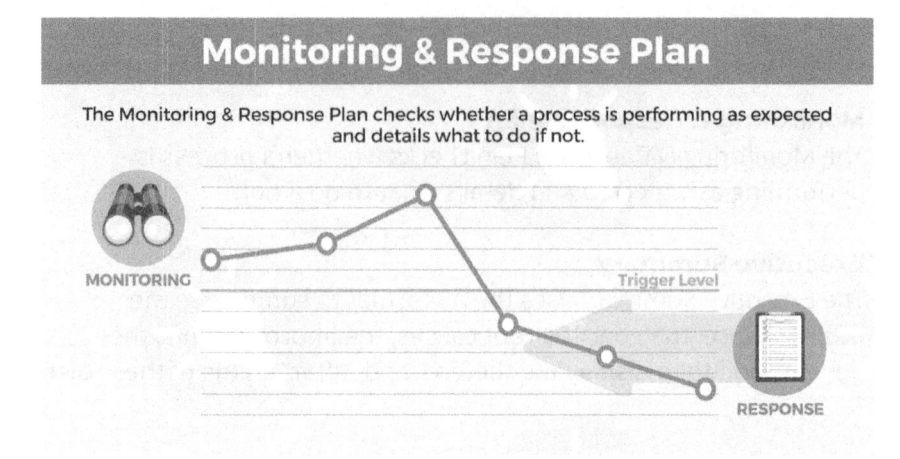

Monitoring & Response Plan

Monitoring & Response Plan

The Monitoring & Response Plan checks whether a process is performing as expected and details what to do if not.

MONITORING

Trigger Level

RESPONSE

What is a Monitoring & Response Plan?

A Monitoring Plan is a data collection plan for checking the ongoing health of the improved process. It lists the measures, the targets for each measure, how each measure will be checked and who will check the measures. It sets the stage for the Response Plan.

The Response Plan establishes a threshold or trigger level for each measure in the Monitoring Plan. When the process performance goes beyond a trigger level, the Response Plan details immediate and long-term actions that will help the process return to and maintain the desired performance.

What Questions Will a Monitoring & Response Plan Answer?

- Which measures should be continually monitored?
- What's the desired level of performance?
- Who's going to collect this data and how often?
- How low or high can the performance go before we react?

- Who's responsible for responding to the drop in performance?
- What is the response plan?

Example of a Monitoring & Response Plan

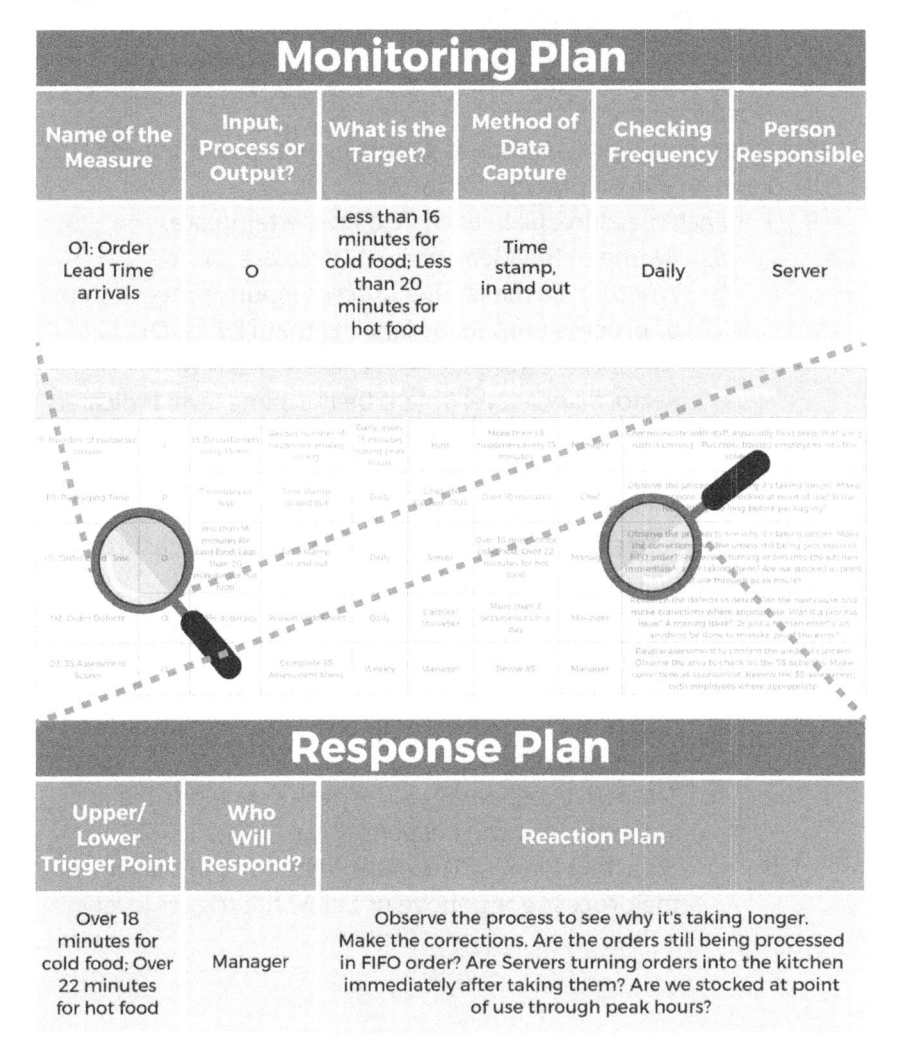

Monitoring Plan

Name of the Measure	Input, Process or Output?	What is the Target?	Method of Data Capture	Checking Frequency	Person Responsible
O1: Order Lead Time arrivals	O	Less than 16 minutes for cold food; Less than 20 minutes for hot food	Time stamp, in and out	Daily	Server

Response Plan

Upper/ Lower Trigger Point	Who Will Respond?	Reaction Plan
Over 18 minutes for cold food; Over 22 minutes for hot food	Manager	Observe the process to see why it's taking longer. Make the corrections. Are the orders still being processed in FIFO order? Are Servers turning orders into the kitchen immediately after taking them? Are we stocked at point of use through peak hours?

[Download Template] The main measure to keep an eye on is the Order Lead Time. If the timestamps show lead times going above 16 minutes for cold food or 20 minutes for hot food then it's time for the manager to check if anyone is reverting to old behaviors like Last-In-First-Out or holding on to orders too long. It's important to watch and make corrections until the new process is second nature to everyone.

Roadside Assistance
How to Create a Monitoring & Response Plan

1. Download the Monitoring and Response Plan template.
2. Determine which measures should be monitored in order to keep an eye on process performance.
3. For each measure, fill in each field on the template:
    a. "Name of the Measures" — These are short
    b. Whether it's measuring process inputs, process steps or process outputs by labeling them I, P or O
    c. "What is the Target?" — This is the desired performance level (might be the same level indicated in the Goal Statement).
    d. "The Method of Capture" — How the data will be collected (i.e Check Sheets, system reports, etc.)
    e. "Checking Frequency" — How often this measure will be collected
    f. "Person Responsible" — Who'll be collecting this data (the more automated the better)
    g. "Upper/Lower Trigger Level — If the process goes higher or lower than these levels the the Response Plan goes into effect
    h. "Who Will Respond?" — The person responsible for implementing the Response Plan
    i. "Reaction Plan" — The steps to put into action once the process goes above or below the trigger level

Potholes and Detours Around Them

Potholes	Detours
Not listing the Project Y on the plan	If there is only one measure to continue monitoring it would be the Project Y. That is the minimum of what goes on the Monitoring & Response Plan.
Hitting the Trigger level frequently and putting Response Plan into effect all the time	Make sure the Trigger level isn't set too close to typical process performance. Control Limits from a Control Chart often make the best trigger levels since those are above and below the normal process variation.

Sightseeing and Additional References

Template:
- Monitoring & Response Plan

Webinar:
- How to Build a Powerful Project Storyboard

FROM THE TRAVEL KIT:

Executive Summary (aka Completed A3)

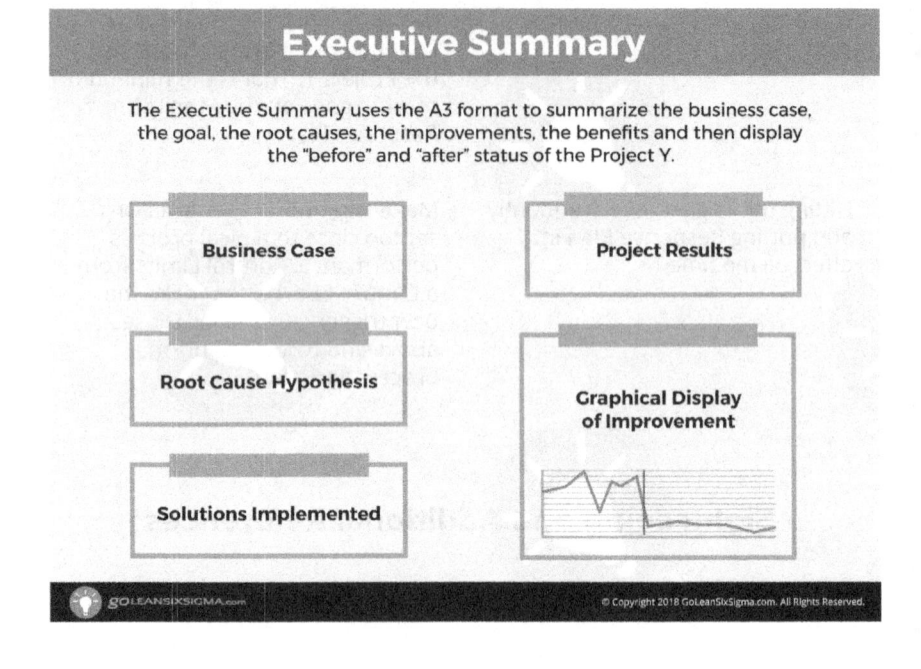

Executive Summary

The Executive Summary uses the A3 format to summarize the business case, the goal, the root causes, the improvements, the benefits and then display the "before" and "after" status of the Project Y.

- Business Case
- Root Cause Hypothesis
- Solutions Implemented
- Project Results
- Graphical Display of Improvement

© Copyright 2018 GoLeanSixSigma.com. All Rights Reserved.

What is an Executive Summary?

The Executive Summary is an overview of a Lean Six Sigma project for leadership which highlights the findings and improvements. This one-page template summarizes the original business case, the project goal, a list of findings/improvements and a tally of the total project gains. The results featured are a mix of increased revenue, decreased costs, decreased cycle time, decreased waste, and increased customer satisfaction along with a Run Chart of the before and after state of the Project Y or main metric. This summary is customarily the first page of either a Storyboard or an Executive Report of a completed improvement project.

What Questions Will an Executive Summary Answer?

- What is the one-page story of the improvement effort?
- What's a good way to share the story of this project with busy people?

Example of an Executive Summary

Business Case
Cycle Time improvement in our food orders for lunch would result in an enhanced client experience. Cycle Time improvement could also translate into monetary benefits because we may turn tables quicker and seat more customers, which will increase revenue.

Project Results
- Order Lead Time has reduced from 28 minutes to 15 minutes
- Sandwich Lead Time dropped from 14 to 10 minutes on average
- Customers reporting higher levels of satisfaction
- Lunch order volume has increased 18%

Root Cause Analysis
Data showed sandwich prep time took too long, lots of time spent searching for items, prep area is disorganized, not stocking enough of key items and running out during noon rush and packaging process is disorganized and causing pick-up delays.

Graphical Display of Improvement
Improved Order Lead Time

Solutions Implemented
1. Created new order form - Standard Work
2. Created a Work Cell in the prep area
3. Used Takt Time to create Workload Balance in the kitchen
4. Created a Just-In-Time system with Kanbans
5. Conducted 5S in prep area (ongoing audits)
6. Added labels to bins for visual management
7. Conducted Cross-Training for front of house flexibility

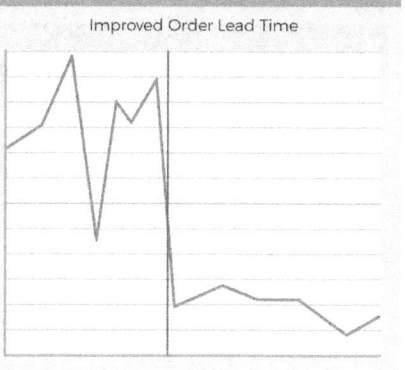

[Download Template] Since the team had been updating and sharing the A3 throughout the project, it was easy to update it and create the Executive Summary. They were happy to include the Run Chart showing such impressive improvement in the Lunch Order Lead Time.

Roadside Assistance
How to Create an Executive Summary

1. Download the Executive Summary template.
2. Summarize the:
   a. Business Case.
   b. Root Causes.
   c. Implemented countermeasures (provide a bulleted list).
   d. Resulting time and cost savings along with customer impact.
3. Insert a Run Chart displaying the before and after status of the Project Y (main metric).

Potholes and Detours Around Them

Potholes	Detours
Not making the purpose of the project clear	Make sure the Business Case makes it clear "why" this project was important — how bad was it?
Not including all the improvements	Be sure to list every change made in a bulleted list — you want to show the many improvements made.
Only listing the change to the Project Y in the results	Be sure to include all the impacts and outcomes of the project — you deserve credit!
Not including a visual of the "before" and "after" status of the Project Y	A picture is worth a 1,000 words so include the Run Chart!

Sightseeing and Additional References

Template:
- Executive Summary

Webinar:
- How to Build a Powerful Project Storyboard

FROM THE TRAVEL KIT:
Project Storyboard

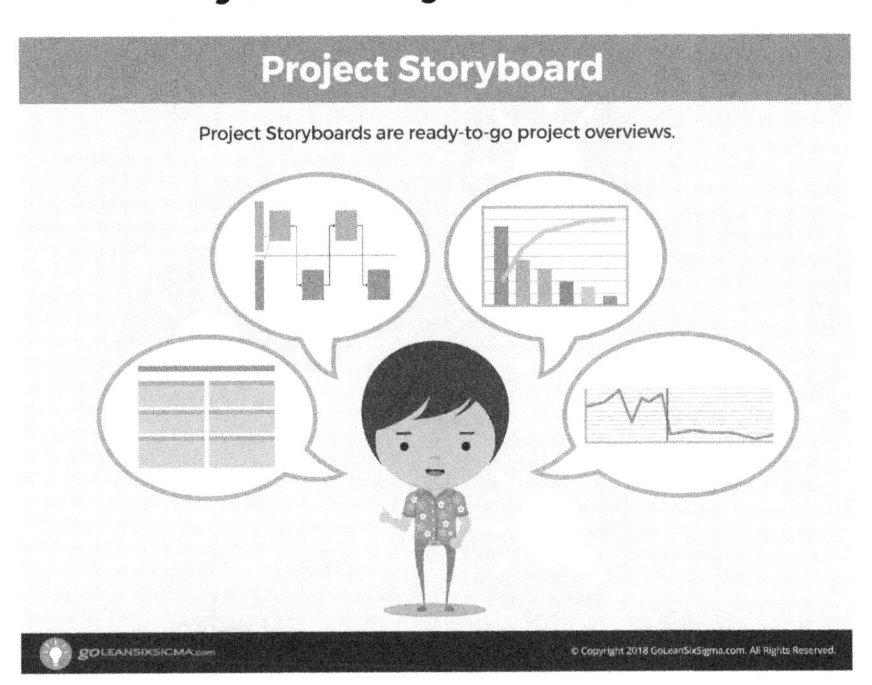

Project Storyboard

Project Storyboards are ready-to-go project overviews.

What is a Project Storyboard?

Project Storyboards are ready-to-go project overviews. They communicate the success stories of process improvement projects and serve as examples of real-world application of Lean Six Sigma. Storyboards also share lessons learned so that others can replicate success and avoid common pitfalls.

What Questions Will a Project Storyboard Answer?

- What did this project accomplish?
- How will the customers, employees and organization benefit?
- How does the end result compare to the baseline?
- What are the hard and soft savings?
- What lessons did the team learn?
- Can this success be applied somewhere else?

Example of a Project Storyboard

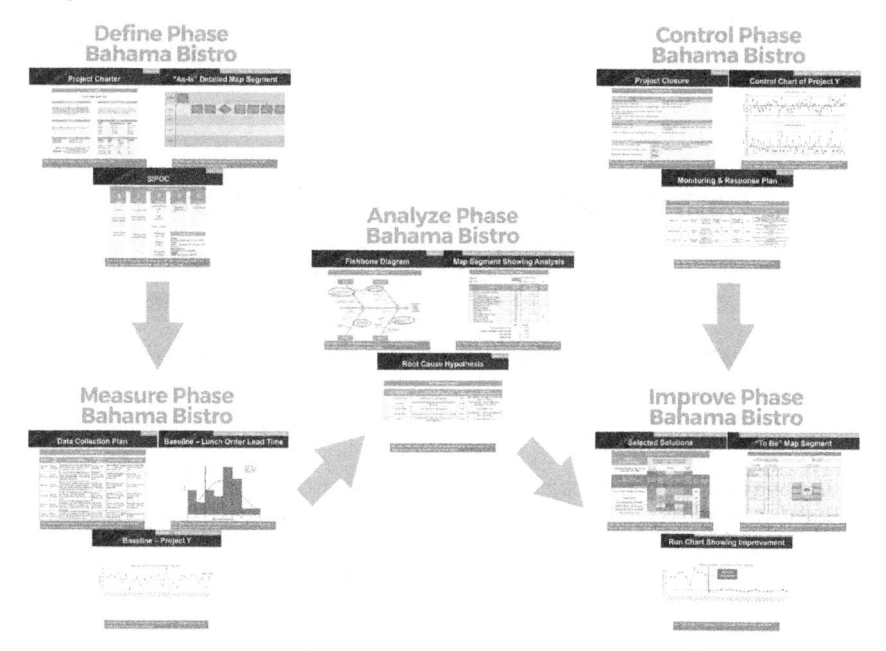

Define Phase — Bahama Bistro

Measure Phase — Bahama Bistro

Analyze Phase — Bahama Bistro

Improve Phase — Bahama Bistro

Control Phase — Bahama Bistro

[Download Template] The Executive Summary was great for most stakeholders but the team put together a Storyboard of all their work so they could help educate other improvement teams. It was great to include lessons learned so no one else had to repeat their mistakes!

Roadside Assistance
How to Create a Project Storyboard

1. Download the Storyboard template.
2. Enter the project title and your name on the cover slide.
3. Cut and paste key project work into the Storyboard.
    a. See Bahama Bistro examples for what to include.
    b. Follow the DMAIC order as suggested.
    c. Refer to Storyboard Checklist (in Storyboard Template) for recommended elements.
4. Add a "Take Away" to each slide to explain what the team learned from the the tool, template or chart.

5. Be sure the presentation tells the "story" of the project on its own.
6. Add any extra slides, charts, graphs and templates to the Appendix.
7. Get feedback from the team and Project Sponsor/Champion and adjust contents as advised.

Potholes and Detours Around Them

Potholes	Detours
Using tiny text in the template that is too hard to read	Enlarge text on templates before inserting into PowerPoint template.
Cutting and pasting templates with hard-to-read formatting	Check instructions in Storyboard template for what cut & paste methods work best for PC or Mac platforms.
Not including a chart of the Project Y	Charts and graphs must be created in either Excel or a stats package such as MiniTab, SigmaXL or others.
Lacking clarity on what a given tool or chart meant to the project	Be sure to include a "Take Away" at the bottom of each slide to explain what was learned.

Sightseeing and Additional References

Templates:
- Green Belt Project Storyboard
- Black Belt Project Storyboard

Webinar:
- How to Build a Powerful Project Storyboard

HELP WITH THE TRAVEL KIT:

Innovation Transfer

One of the great advantages of having used the tools and documented your work is that you can apply the learning and the results elsewhere. Is there another process in the organization that could benefit from your work? Is there another department with the same process, the same problem and maybe even the same root cause?

Transferring solutions accomplishes lots of great things. It spreads success, it saves time and effort and it educates others about the joys of problem solving. Take a moment to consider where else you could apply what you and your team accomplished.

HELP WITH THE TRAVEL KIT:

The Next Project

What's next? What problems did you see along the way? What else needs fixing? Even the process you just fixed could be improved. Remember, process improvement is "continuous." You and your crew are bonafide problem-solvers now and problem-solving is the life blood of great organizations.

You've completed maintenance on your successful process change so maybe it's time for a new car? Something sporty? With every effort, you get better and faster at process improvement. Fasten your seatbelts and get in gear!

Control Phase: Summary

Nice job! Way to hang in there and see it through! This isn't the end but it's a great stop point. If you feel like sharing the good news, we'd love to hear your story. Check out some other project success stories here and reach out if you'd like to join the ranks of other successful problem solvers.

It's been a great trip and we know you're looking forward to continuing down this road. Check out our concluding thoughts as you take out your map to plan your next adventure.

Control Phase Challenges

- Making sure improvements are ingrained before team members move on to "fixing" another process
- Standardizing the documentation
- Continuing the monitoring necessary to ensure adherence to the new process
- Maintaining the discipline required to complete the Control Phase

Control Phase Best Practices

- Make monitoring visible and accessible to those who do the work.
- Include process participants in monitoring — hand-drawn charts & tables are fine.
- Don't leave key pieces out of the Storyboard — check that it tells the "story."
- Include the Process Owner in the Control Plan well in advance of the handoff.

Journey Journaling

Tired? Want someone else to take the wheel? Time for just a few last questions:
- Are you proud?
- Is the team proud? Project Champion? Process Owner?

- Did you communicate your project success broadly?
- What final lessons did you learn?
- What would you do differently next time? Ready?

Control Phase Journey

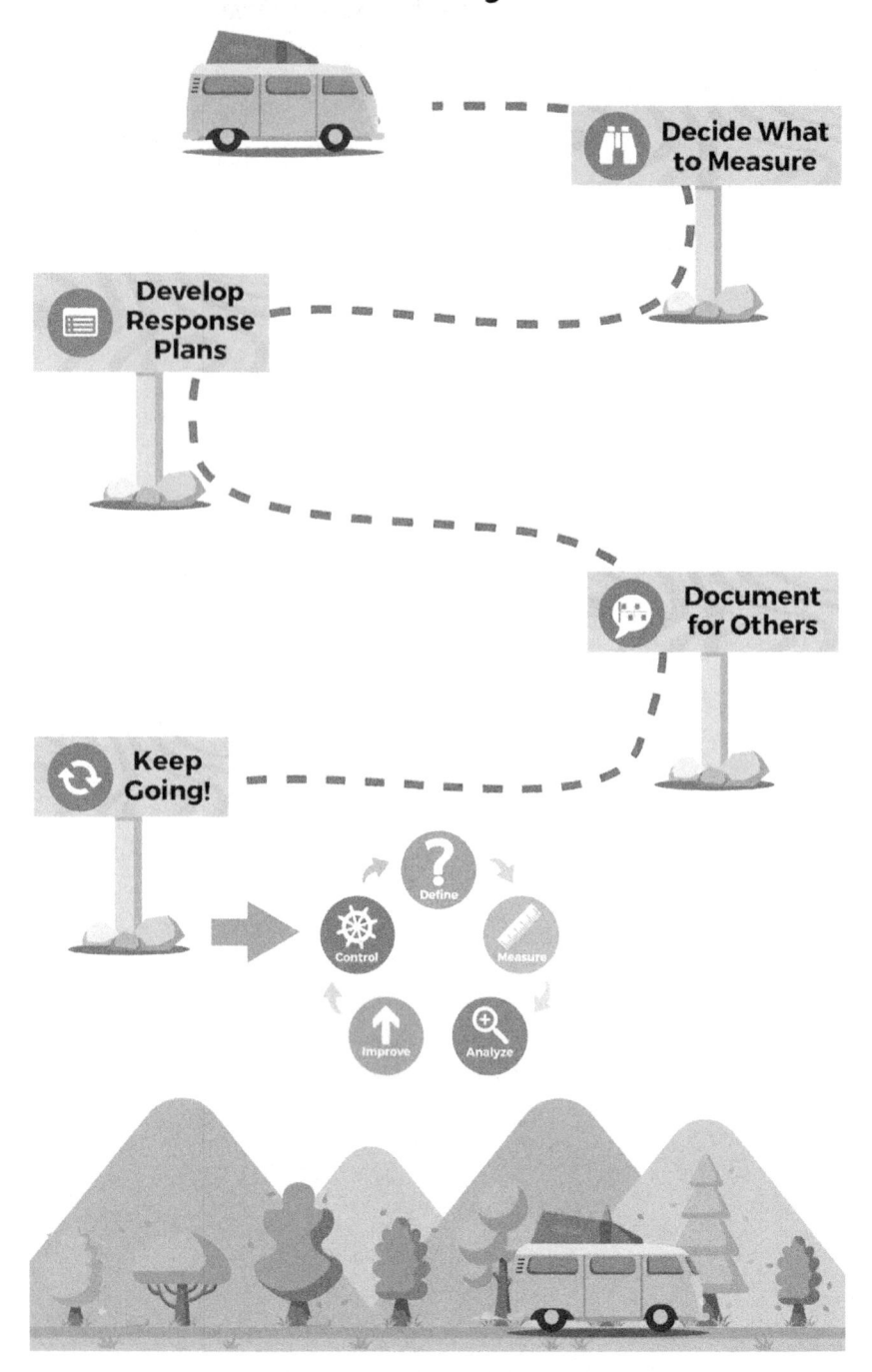

- Decide What to Measure
- Develop Response Plans
- Document for Others
- Keep Going!

"Life is a journey, not a destination."
— Ralph Waldo Emerson

Congratulations! You've come to the end of a perfectly lovely DMAIC journey. You're energized and motivated to…take more road trips! Big wins, small fixes; this could be the start of a life-long relationship — and a beautiful friendship — with process improvement.

The roadmap is a great framework for your travels, but not every problem follows the same route. You may revisit certain phases multiple times before moving forward, and that's OK! As you get more problem-solving experience, you'll take detours and occasionally follow the road less travelled. Again, that's OK. There's lots more to see and do. Are you ready for some off-roading?

Here are five things to do between road trips to strengthen and tone your problem-solving muscles. Keep these top of mind:

1. Maintain Your New Skills

Make a commitment to apply and maintain your new process improvement skills. Don't wait. Keep training your process improvement eyes to see waste and remove it. Start a project right away or take another turn with the process you just improved. Even if your organization doesn't require more improvements, make a commitment to yourself.

2. Help Build a Culture of Continuous Improvement

Use your new skills to generate enthusiasm, fun and recognition. It is truly amazing what people can accomplish with continuous improvement, and sharing those stories builds a supportive culture. Find opportunities to bring people together to share, collaborate and celebrate success.

3. Engage in the Continuous Improvement Community

There's a huge network of problem solvers out there. Conferences that cater exclusively to continuous improvement abound. Reach out, attend and participate! You'll be inspired and energized, and you may inspire others, too.

4. Become a Peer Coach and Mentor Others

You don't have to be an expert to share what you've learned with your peers. Teach them your new-found concepts and tools. Teaching others is one of the best ways to deepen your own understanding. Asking people to share where they are in their improvement journey is a great place to start.

5. Pursue Your Education

Being a lifelong learner is incredibly gratifying. There are new webinars, blogs, podcasts and videos coming out every day. Set a reminder and challenge yourself to learn something new once a month, once a week, every day! Treat yourself to something as quick as a 10-second infographic, read a 2-minute blog, sign up for a 1-hour webinar or pursue the next level of training. You deserve it.

We expect to see you out there on the road since you'll never stop learning!

Acknowledgements

As with any endeavor, you're never really doing it on your own. Even if you don't ask for help, your parents must have done something right if you've written a book! That said, we'd like to thank the people who made this book better than it would have been.

First and foremost, we want to acknowledge Julius Pecson. Julius is the Operations Director at GoLeanSixSigma.com and the three of us collaborated on each and every infographic. Did the image convey the thought? Was the definition clear? He was not only our graphic partner, he was another set of eyes and a wealth of imagination.

Credit is also due to Sion Lee, Managing Partner and Chief Technical Officer here at GoLeanSixSigma.com. Sion invented the joyful Bistro Staff and the tempting environs of the Bahama Bistro. Together, Sion and Julius supplied the graphic wonder.

We were also lucky to have a generous team of reviewers. We reached out to users, project managers, Master Black Belts, authors, educators and industry thought leaders. We'd like to give a shout out to John Guaspari, author of *Otherwise Engaged*, for performing what he called "The Full Grundy" on our first draft. Aside from highlighting every missing period and misplaced pronoun, he had wonderful insights and humorous asides. Although he accused us of being "serial comma killers," we're all still friends.

We want to thank Karyn Ross, co-author of *The Toyota Way to Service Excellence* for her invaluable suggestions from the Lean side of the house. Jerry Wright, former head of Association for Manufacturing Excellence (AME) also gave us excellent food for thought. Bill Zerter from our Advisory Board probably sacrificed a perfectly good Sunday thinking about how we could do better.

One of GoLeanSixSigma.com's Master Black Belts, Bill Eureka, gave us a whole new set of potholes to think about — thanks for those! And Dodd Starbird of Implementation Partners had some good fun with our metaphors. Big thanks to our Client Experience Managers, Anna Comia and Kelvin Tanjuakio for keeping the business cranking and humming with excitement while we disappeared into the digital writing "shed."

We'd like to serve a big bowl of appreciation to CEO Karlo Tanjuakio — our "Nudger-In-Chief" — who said, "Why don't you guys write a book?" Suddenly there was a timeline, an ambitious to-do list and lots of emails asking, "How's the book coming?" Nothing would have happened without you Karlo — thank you.

And lastly, we want to thank all of the problem-solvers we've had the pleasure of teaching, coaching and mentoring over the decades. We want to acknowledge the students who embraced, loved and voraciously pursued process improvement. We're honored you looked to us for guidance.

As you were busy learning about the tools, we got to learn more about how to mentor, guide and teach. You gave us a gift and helped us to make the learning process easier, better and way more fun. Thank you!

Index

5 Whys	135-137
Template	137
Webinars	137
Single Module Training	137
5S	147-150
Templates	150
Webinar	150
Single Module Training	150
8 Wastes	33-36
Check Sheet Template	36
Single Module Training	36
A3	71-75
Template	75
Webinar on coaching with A3	75
Analyze Phase	108-143
Baseline Measure	102-105
Box Plot	125-127
How to create using Minitab or SigmaXL	127
Webinar on creating charts and graphs	127
Champion (Sponsor)	41-43
Check Sheet	98-101
Template	101
Coaching with A3 Webinar	75
Control Phase	167-184
Customer Value Checklist Template	56
Cycle Time, Measures of	95-97
Data Collection Plan	85-89
Template	88
Webinar	89
Define Phase	47-81
DMAIC	19, 24, 28-29, 39, 72
Executive Summary	174-177
Template	177
Failure Modes & Effects Analysis (FMEA)	160-164
Template	164

Webinar	164
Single Module Training	164
Fishbone Diagram	131-134
Template	134
Webinar	134
Single Module Training	134
FMEA (Failure Modes & Effects Analysis)	160-164
Template	164
Webinar	164
Single Module Training	164
Goal Statement Builder Template	53
Green Belt Training, Getting Started Webinar	40
Histogram	119-121
How to create in Minitab or SigmaXL	121
Webinar on creating charts and graphs	121
Single Module Training	121
Impact Effort Matrix Template	40
Improve Phase	144-166
Improvement Team	44
Innovation Transfer	181
Kanban	154-156
Lead Time	95-97
Leader Support Webinar	43
Lean, Introduction Webinar	36
Lean Six Sigma	23-25
Project Types	30
Measure Phase	82-106
Monitoring & Response Plan	170-173
Template	173
Operational Definition	89-91
Template	88
Ohno, Taiichi	36
Pareto Chart	116-119
How to create in Minitab or SigmaXL	118
Webinar on creating charts and graphs	119
PDCA	24-27, 29, 72
Process Time	95-97
Process Walk	60-64
Video	64
Planning Checklist	64

Interview Sheet	64
Planning Webinar	64
Single Module Training	64
Facilitation Webinar	64
Project Champion (Sponsor)	41-43
Project Charter	50-53
Single Module Training	53
Template	53
Project Maturity Stages	40
Project Screener Template	40
Project Selection	37-40
Guide Template	40
Project Sponsor (Champion)	41-43
Project Storyboard	177-180
Template	180
Webinar	180
Project Types	30
Response Plan	170-173
Root Cause Hypothesis Statement	138-141
Template	141
Run Chart	122-124
How to create using Minitab or SigmaXL	124
Webinar on creating charts and graphs	124
Scatter Plot	128-130
How to create using Minitab or SigmaXL	130
Webinar on creating charts and graphs	130
SIPOC	57-60
Webinar	60
Single Module Training	60
Solution Selection Matrix	157-159
Template	159
Spaghetti Map Template	153
Sponsor (Champion)	41-43
Stakeholder Analysis	75-78
Storyboard, Project	177-180
Template	180
Webinar	180
Swimlane Map	64-67
Template	67
Single Module Training	67

Takt Time	92-94
Value-Added Flow Analysis	111-115
Template	115
Value Stream Map	68-71, 96-97
Template	71
Single Module Training	71
Voice of the Customer Translation Matrix	53-56
Template	56
Wait Time	95-97
Work Cell Design	151-153

Made in the USA
Middletown, DE
21 June 2019